The Athletic Development
of the Dressage Horse

ALSO BY CHARLES DE KUNFFY

Dressage Questions Answered
Creative Horsemanship

The Athletic Development of the Dressage Horse
Manege Patterns

Charles de Kunffy

Howell Book House
New York

Maxwell Macmillan Canada
Toronto

Maxwell Macmillan International
New York   Oxford   Singapore   Sydney

Howell Book House   Maxwell Macmillan Canada, Inc.
Macmillan Publishing Company   1200 Eglinton Avenue East
866 Third Avenue   Suite 200
New York, NY 10022   Don Mills, Ontario M3C 3N1

Macmillan Publishing Company is part of the Maxwell Communication Group of Companies.

Library of Congress Cataloging-in-Publication Data

De Kunffy, Charles
    The athletic development of the dressage horse : manege patterns
/ Charles de Kunffy.
        p.   cm.
    Includes index.
    ISBN 0-87605-896-9
    1. Dressage horses—Training.   I. Title.
SF309.6.D45   1992
799.2'3—dc20   92-3327
                                                                                    CIP

All illustrations are by the author unless otherwise credited.

Macmillan books are available at special discounts for bulk purchases for sales promotions, premiums, fund-raising, or educational use. For details, contact:

Special Sales Director
Macmillan Publishing Company
866 Third Avenue
New York, NY 10022

10   9   8   7   6   5   4   3
Printed in the United States of America

Contents

Acknowledgments

Everyone credited with photographic or graphic and design work in the pages of this book earned my deepest gratitude. They helped with enthusiasm and made my compilation of this manuscript not only possible but a pleasure.

My great appreciation to Herr Arthur Kottas-Heldenberg, Chief Rider of the Spanish Riding School in Vienna, Austria, cannot be sufficiently expressed. His pictures bring excellence and elegance to this modest book. The effort to have them made and sent to me was considerable, yet done so gracefully as if it were natural to toil for the betterment of my text. One of the greatest riders in the world, and one of the busiest, granted me an unparalleled privilege.

My gratitude to Mr. Andreas Jarc of Vienna, Austria, and Mr. Richard Williams of California is special. They contributed pictures for the jacket of this book, and through their art the book will be visually attractive to all who seek it out.

Richard Williams also contributed many of the beautifully executed illustrations and his excellent photographs. While his artistic contributions might thus be obvious to the reader, I must add that Richard's contribution through inspired equestrian conversations helped develop the themes and the taxonomy of this volume. He fine-combed the manuscript to verify correct expression of meaning.

Dr. Reiner Klimke, with his proverbial generosity, permitted a photograph of his tempi-changes during his Victory Round on the occasion of winning the Los Angeles Olympics to be included. All who look at this book will now share in that glorious moment. The symbolic power of this picture will speak to all equestrians who ride with their intellect and spirit.

Mr. and Mrs. Paul Drake, one taking the photographs, the other gracing them, have responded promptly, generously and with their usual quality of the "product" they donated to this book. They were the first to do so and gave me courage, without which there are no other virtues.

Ms. Barbara Leistico gave much more than the excellent graphics for illustrations. She worked overtime and on some weekends to complete them. To do so much work, and to do it during sacred leisure hours, is work that cannot be thanked enough.

I have been the recipient of many people's largesse in helping me to complete this book. But I must remind my readers that my thoughts come from my devoted riding teachers, all masters of the art, who gave me whatever knowledge I can pass on. Equally indebted am I to all of my riding students, who allowed me to think about equestrian matters and who allowed me to learn from their needs perhaps more than I could teach them.

My greatest appreciation, however, is reserved for Mrs. Madelyn Larsen, Senior Editor. She encouraged the speedy completion of this manuscript and facilitated its acceptance by the publisher. During my writing and editing, she gave me advice, encouragement and enthusiasm. She edited my manuscript in a way remarkable both for the quantity and the quality of her work. Every line needed doctoring and she found all the troubles from spelling to syntax. More remarkably, she edited so knowledgeably that the contents remained unchanged and I needed to do no more than approve her changes. If she were a rider, she would be one of the most scholastically knowledgeable ones.

She has a great command of the subject and a thoroughness in editing that I have never seen before.

Kindness, efficiency, praise, were given during my work and her help has not even ended as I write these words of appreciation. Without her, this manuscript would not be now in print.

Preface

I am not aware of any book, other than this one, that focuses on the meaning of the patterns we ride in a manege. After teaching and lecturing on the subject of classical horsemanship for decades, I believe a book such as this will be indispensable to the serious rider. I say this for two reasons.

First, now that most riding academies have closed their doors, only a few institutions remain that still teach courses of adequate duration (2 to 4 years) for the proper training of equitation. Consequently, the knowledge of the acceptable manege patterns and the particular usefulness of each is rapidly diminishing and gradually disappearing.

Second, the growing interest in classical horsemanship is concurrent with the ever diminishing supply of experts who can pass on to a new generation this vast and wonderful tradition uncorrupted. As the demand by far outdistances the supply of correct equestrian knowledge, books gain an exaggerated importance in filling this vacuum.

I sincerely hope that by passing on some of my knowledge, experiences and insights regarding the legitimacy and usefulness of manege patterns, I can significantly contribute to the reader's success in schooling horses that remain sound, healthy and happy. Such horses do their work with ease and therefore are a great pleasure to ride.

Introduction

While this book may specifically focus on the meaning and use-fulness of patterns in riding, it is also a book about the proper training of horses in the respected dressage tradition. Therefore it is very important to explain general training principles briefly before becoming pattern-specific.

To be sure that patterns are discussed and understood in the proper training context, I must ease the reader toward them by outlining briefly the major principles guiding all training for the gymnastic improvement of horses.

THE HORSE'S DEVELOPMENTAL POTENTIALITIES

Both heredity and environment have roles in determining the horse's ultimate performance and gymnastic achievements. Thus, we must pay attention to both factors in order to select a sports horse wisely and to train him properly by adhering to traditionally accepted training procedures. *Heredity* determines the maximum limits of the individual's possibilities for athletic development. The limitations of the genetic package cannot be overcome by even the best training philosophy, carried out by the best trainer. *Environmental influences* will determine how much of the hereditary potentialities will be displayed in actual performance. While the environmental influences, including training, cannot create better performance than is genetically predetermined, they are responsible for maximizing the display of the hereditary potentialities.

The following is an outline of the major features of these two influential elements that interact in the determination of the horse's athletic performance.

Heredity/Nature

CONFORMATION The structure of the horse has to be correct for optimal motion and powerful locomotion. Also, an ideal balance and correct place for the center of gravity depend on the structure and its proportions. By all means the horse should look as if it could be picked up (by the fingers of an imaginary giant) just behind its elbows and hang there with head and tail in perfect equilibrium while remaining level with (parallel to) the ground.

SOUNDNESS The legs, which provide the "underpinnings" and locomotion, should be healthy and strong. Equally important is that all four legs be straight when viewed from the front and rear and that the front legs be straight also from a side view. While horses with such requirements are not in the majority, we must make our selection even more difficult by insisting that the horse also moves his legs straight. Pendulum-like, forward swinging of the legs, with no tolerance for crossing, winging, paddling and other compromises of the straight and forward action of the legs, is paramount. The respiration and the heart of any sports horse need strengthening, but in order to qualify as a prospect, the horse must have perfectly formed legs.

TEMPERAMENT The prospect should be alert but not nervous or fidgety. He should be attentive rather than scatterbrained and easily distracted. He should concentrate yet not be stubborn. He should display a willing nature but without initiating. And prize

Often while instructing I have to ride a completely strange horse in order to demonstrate to the rider how one does things to make a horse improve.

Here I am riding a horse that had mostly Western training and would not flex longitudinally toward the bit. Muscles tense, skeletally stiff, he moved above the bit uncomfortably with tiny steps that lacked any suspension. I had to ride him to help him change and also to give his rider feedback and teach her what longitudinal flexion feels like.

Ten minutes after I rode this willing stranger, he is flexed, attentive, yet relaxed and moves with rhythmic, elevated and very well-synchronized (diagonal pairs of legs) strides. None of which was forthcoming before I sat on him. To do this is never easy, but the horse's gratitude for being allowed to carry the rider in comfort is evident even after these few minutes of riding him.   Photo: Susan Sexton.

sensitivity that is without fear! The horse should want to go and offer to sustain locomotion without prodding.

ATHLETIC ABILITY   The horse should have fluent, large gaits and in the trot and canter a great deal of suspension by virtue of loose ligaments and fine coordination. Strong, yet elastic musculature and strong but supple joints are great assets.

Environment/Nurture

GROWTH   Development through motion (and not by food alone) is essential for the horse, which is nature's fine design of a great moving structure.

EQUINE COMPANIONSHIP   The horse is a herd animal that is most inspired to move by his companions. He also needs to be part of a herd in order to become a horse rather than a physical and mental invalid. He must play, fight, contest for a place among his fellows and be stimulated by other horses.

HUMAN PARTNERSHIP   A good relationship, particularly with his trainer, should be established from the first day on. The horse should be handled kindly and be introduced to both equipment and work gradually. He should approach people and come willingly when called. He should show curiosity and trust in people and find joy in their company.

One

The Relevance of Dressage Riding in Horsemanship

Dressage goals, simply stated, include all training activities that prolong the working life and serviceability of the majority of horses. These goals have their origins in guidelines developed by the practical daily working of horses based on trial and error. Classical, or enduring, principles of horsemanship were born of this. Only those riding strategies which produced the desired longevity of the horse and the extension of his working years were retained. These strategies prevail not because human nature is necessarily sweet, benevolent and wise, but because it is often greedy and selfish enough to recognize and covet cheap technology. For millennia the horse was the major technology because of his ability to accelerate the speed by which men could travel, to multiply the strength of his labors and to transport burdens heavier than men could bear. All technology caters to mankind's insatiable appetite for ease and inertia. That is why all the inventions that save energy or time become successes. The history of successful inventions is therefore the history of a lazy humankind's quest for leisure and repose.

To his speed, charmingly and coincidentally, nature added superb elegance and uplifting grandeur to the horse. Even at a standstill the horse is a monument to beauty, and therefore was coveted by kings and emperors, as much as any throne. Many public monuments, consequently, immortalize the powerful enthroned on a horse. For a horse can elevate and dignify an already august presence.

By their legendary work we know the historical masters of horsemanship. From their recommendations we can glean a common denominator: They were animated by a great love for the horse. Their kind of sophisticated love was rooted in the desire to promote the well-being of the horse. They did not associate with horses for self-aggrandizement. Their mature love for the horse was based on their desire to serve him well, to cater to his, not to human, needs. This emotion inevitably defines the logical goal of all classical equitation: to explore and unfold the nature-given potentialities of each horse to its fullest.

Briefly surveying the fundamental principles guiding dressage riding, we can summarize them as follows:

The partnership between horse and rider is difficult to achieve and even more ambitious to make beneficial to both. Horse and rider possess the two most unlikely anatomies to be harmoniously united for the purpose of progressing effortlessly through space. The horse has a narrow, precariously balanced, horizontal structure, much like a pipeline. This structure has narrowly set, weak underpinnings, the legs, bridged by a weak back. There, almost at its weakest point, the most unlikely candidate for partnership, the vertically pipelike human, wishes to intercept at a 90-degree angle. Both are creatures of precarious balance, even when left alone to cope with the ground. In riding, we wish to harmonize our balance with the horse's for common progress through space. The unsteady "horizontal pipe" of the horse is supposed to carry in perfect balance and harmony his struggling-to-find-his-balance rider, the "vertical pipe." The horse's structure makes no provisions for carrying any added weight on his back. Neither the skeleton nor the musculature of the horse suggest any weight-bearing tolerance, let alone ability. Therefore, from the moment that we arrive in the saddle, we must spend a lifetime apologizing for having gotten there.

The horse's natural impaction on the ground, when he travels over it, is traumatized by the excess weight of the rider on his back. Each step made under the rider's foreign weight has the potential to cause discomfort, pain and ultimately damage to the horse. Nor is the rider spared! For he places himself on a potential cement breaker, pelvic pulverizer, brain scrambler and dislodger of kidney stones. Yet, there is no cause for pessimism. For the knowledgeable rider knows that the horse can carry him effortlessly in balance once the rider has an independent seat made adhesive by the proper lumbar following motion. And every horse can carry himself effortlessly when induced by his rider to flex and stretch longitudinally. Thus, discomfort, pain and injury can be, and should be, avoided in an equine-human partnership. Knowledge of how to create the physiological circumstances under which motion in unity can prosper, be uninjurious and a source of pleasure is the task of scholarly equitation that produces the art of riding.

The partnership between horse and rider should be developed beyond a state of reducing mutual discomfort and injury. It should reach the kind of perfection in unity and partnership that the horse and rider will appear to an observer as if they are animated by an outside force. Communication between them should be imperceptible. Motion, much like in a dancing partnership, should appear to be voluntary and pleasurable to both participants.

Horsemen of understanding and insight know that the beauty of the horse unfolds and increases only if he is improved through his own virtues and talents. The art in horsemanship must be perceived only as a verification and a fulfillment of its object, the horse. Before beauty emerges, the "definitive virtues" (the things that define the art object) must be developed. If horses can be defined by their virtues of swiftness, agility and strength on the one hand and patience, loyalty, attention and memory on the other, then their beauty is enhanced when these "definitive virtues" are cultivated.

Both the riding skills and controls of the equestrian and the athletic skills of the horse should be simultaneously and habitually cultivated. The rider should analyze every day whether his equitation has improved since the day before. He should also inquire whether the horse's needs have been better served this day than on the preceding one. By consistently maintaining high standards in daily work, both partners will perform with the ease only habituality can lend to unerring performance. For the art of riding, much like the other performing arts, depends on a lack of self-consciousness about the fundamental skills on which it is established.

The pleasure in riding should be found in seeking, not finding, perfection. For all wise equestrians have known that our ideals are not fully attainable, only approachable. Horsemanship is an art not suitable to those who wish to "arrive." It is, rather, an art in which the process of creating is fulfilling. The great German Romantic poet Goethe said that "everybody wants to be somebody; nobody wants to grow." Riders must want to grow. For that process is, indeed, the art. Therefore, in the equestrian arts, the process of daily work must be perfected because that is all that we can ever accomplish. Perfection of riding remains in the quest for it, but it will always elude completion. Riding is, therefore, an ongoing, never-ending, challenging process. That aspect makes riding so intelligent and significant an effort. One merely strives, never arrives.

The equestrian art is without peer and parallel if considered in terms of a "plastic art" with great visual appeal. Beyond the three-dimensionality of sculpture, one finds a fourth dimension: motion. Riding is sculpting while progressing through space. In this respect, it is an art similar to ballet, gymnastics and figure skating. However, our imagination must progress beyond those analogies because we create beauty in motion with an unlikely, living and individually willful partner. The horse has a great bulk and a strong will with instinctually guided determination. Oscar Wilde said that "it is only shallow people who do not judge by appearance." Knowledgeable observers will discern the depth of the art in riding, indeed, by its appearance. For beauty through harmonious partnership in motion will appeal to the senses as well as to the emotions.

The processes of the equestrian art include the following major concepts:

1. The horse's natural potentialities can only be fulfilled by the knowledgeable (based on academic expertise), systematic, gradual and harmonious development of his talents. Only

through the horse's voluntary cooperation and trust in his rider, reinforced by frequent rewarding of his work, can the horse achieve the maximum display of his talents.

2. Dressage, gymnastic work, has to be first and foremost rehabilitative, then therapeutic, and only after these stages make it possible, athletic. The first two stages of work deal with correcting troubles caused by past injuries and man-made aches and pains. Therapeutic work also addresses the never-ending task of making every horse "ambidextrous." Born naturally crooked, one-sided and with a natural inclination toward unequal use of both his musculature and his skeleton, the horse must always be straightened by the rider to prevent injury and breakdown. This effort must include beyond the spinal alignment of the horse over the pattern on which he tracks, the evenly forward loading of his two hind legs. Straightening, of course, is not always geometrically literal. Rather, it refers to the effort of moving the horse always parallel with his spine to the path or pattern of his progression on the ground. So, for instance, straightening a horse when moving on a 20m circle refers to bending his spine evenly and continuously into the identical shape of an arc of the circle. The concept of straightness includes the even use of the two hind legs both in length and height of stride. The motion of the hind legs should be directed toward the hoofprints left by the horse's forehand on the corresponding side.

3. While the preceding two goals may be sufficient for reestablishing the horse's natural balance and freedom of movement under the added weight of the rider, the third concept of good horsemanship calls for athletic development beyond activities the horse would normally volunteer to do. This more sophisticated goal aims to develop the horse to the outmost of his natural inborn potentialities. Yet athletic, gymnastic improvement must remain loyal to the perfection of the natural gaits, the magnification of the natural use of joints and muscles and the amplification of suspension through carriage.

Once the horse is gymnasticized enough to show strength in all the natural gaits, every effort will be made to shift gradually the composite (horse and rider's) center of gravity backward toward the horse's haunches. This effort is called "collection" and allows the horse to move not merely "forward," but to "carry" his rider "forward and upward." Such athletically improved locomotion provides for traversing space in flight well suspended above the ground. Thus percussionary motion by minimum effort produces maximum suspension due to the efficiency and precision of the impaction on the ground. The visual impact is a slow, yet highly animated, motion of the horse carrying his rider softly on a supplely swinging back and on strong but supplely resilient joints that allow him to "stroke the ground" rather than impact on it with a jarring fall. A well-collected horse, somewhat like a mechanical crane, will always be anchored on his haunches, lifting his rider effortlessly to carry him, rather than push him, through space.

Two

Training Strategies

The rider must approach the training of the horse with a very disciplined attitude. Riding must involve the complete attention of both the human and the horse. Submission of the horse to the rider's aids is conditional upon the horse's understanding that his rider is disciplined. That attitude is communicated by the rider's consistency. All desirable qualities should be approved and rewarded and all undesirable activities by the horse should be disapproved of.

Basically, the activity of the rider may involve one of two possible attitudes:

1. The rider may harmonize with whatever the horse is doing, to show his approval by passivity. This maintenance of the status quo is important. The horse will then realize that if he is behaving desirably, his rider will not interfere and alter anything. This sense of harmonious tranquillity is one of the greatest possible rewards for the horse. This is not, however, entirely accomplished by the omission of aids, but rather by the commission of "aids of maintenance," based on gestures that harmonize the rider's balance and move-

ment with that of the horse, to achieve a synchronization of two entities that perpetuates an existing level and quality of cooperation.

2. The rider, if not harmonizing, must disrupt the status quo, but in such a manner as to aid the horse to improve the effort and the situation. In aiding, one has two further options: One can either drive for more activity in the haunches (engagement), or one can half-halt, in order to rebalance the ongoing activity of the horse.

There are two common failings riders exhibit in these matters: From passive (harmonizing) to active (disruptive) aids, the rider should move subtly, smoothly and without disturbing the horse's concentration or his rhythm, which are sophisticated proofs of relaxation. Yet all too often riders cause a major disruption while changing attitudes. Some riders will also either omit or de-emphasize one of the two phases, either that of harmony or that of disruption. Most often harmonizing is omitted or ignored. The horse is bothered and irritated, and not allowed sufficient time for repose as a reward for having done whatever was asked of him. This type of riding produces sour, unhappy, dull and irritated horses that know neither respite nor reward. Such horses lack confidence in the rider's behavior and are frustrated by finding that nothing ever pleases the rider.

Thus, the wise rider will change smoothly from disruptive aids while asking for something new to harmonious and passive behavior as soon as the horse has surrendered to the rider's wishes. Much good comes from the seeming monotony of perpetuating something that is good. If the horse produces, for instance, a fine medium trot, he should be kept moving like that for an extended period of time. The prolongation of the successful performance is always an act of rider approval by harmonization.

Riders should notice and take advantage of actions volunteered by the horse. Horses will often create desirable action unsolicited by their rider. Such action has various causes:

1. Instinctive reactions, such as passaging when excited.
2. Misunderstanding the rider's intentions, for example, in-

stead of departing in canter, extending the trot.

3. Anticipating the rider's wishes by beginning to back from a halt that was intended to be merely sustained.

4. Resisting by taking the wrong lead of canter, for instance. This last circumstance can arise from two origins. Either the horse cannot do physically, because of weakness or inability, what is asked of him, or he cannot understand clearly the rider's aids, which can, of course, be misapplied.

Whichever of the above-mentioned possibilities may be the reason, if a horse makes a move not asked for, the rider often ought to go along with the horse's offering, pretending to the horse that he, the rider, wanted it, thereby reinforcing the impression for the horse that anything allowed to happen is really by the rider's will. This is, of course, opportunistic riding, and such a strategy must be included in proper training options.

A horse that would be constantly contradicted, often punitively, by the rider will soon hesitate to carry out the rider's requests. Such horses will be puzzled by what they perceive to be the rider's inconsistency. They will fear the rider and being punished for not ever knowing for sure whether an aid was really meant or merely perceived. In fact, good trainers will advocate and encourage the horse's initiations and will honor most of them by cooperating with them. Horses, especially at sophisticated levels of education and training, should have the impression that they perform their deeds by themselves and of their own will, for their own pleasure!

Riders should correct their own, not the horse's, behavior first. They should promote mutual trust and analyze the causes of the horse's unplanned behavior. Many unwanted actions by horses are caused, inadvertently, by their riders, particularly by those who still lack a perfectly balanced, independent, adhesive seat. Such riders will unwittingly "shout" their aids and deliver them startlingly without the benefit of preparatory gestures, whereas they should be "whispered."

If the foundation work of the horse is incorrect, nothing will work properly later. Even correct foundation work needs to be reviewed on a daily basis. For instance, if a horse is not straightened and ridden forward evenly at an early stage of his athletic development, all his movements will remain lopsided or crooked. Horses built on crooked foundations will eventually develop unlevel, gimpy, "rein lame" strides. They might even move with constantly crossing legs.

The training or competition figures designed to create or reveal suppleness will but be "painted on" the horse, who in fact will negotiate them with difficulty due to stiffness. Often, so-called advanced horses are so crooked that their basic gaits are impaired, unlevel and impure, and the "figures" they perform are "disfigured" by predictable resistances. Therefore, spending a great deal of time and knowledgeable, honest effort on straightening a horse, and then engaging him to move evenly forward, should be at the heart of each daily training session.

The gymnastic development of the horse should be based on logical, general goals that are well understood. Every day we must ride for the future and not just for that day's pleasure. We should, indeed, endeavor to bring about the utmost development of the inherent potential of each horse. There should also be intermediate goals. These ought to be athletically specific in order to attain certain levels of performance from the horse. Then, there should be very definite daily goals. The rider must remain flexible and alter these daily goals according to the needs that may arise from moment to moment. Goals should just be that, guidelines for our hopes and not braces that we wear on our brains.

Care must be taken that the right athletic goals are pursued and that they give birth to the proper form. All ideal form is born of age-old principles that create the proper athletic goals. The ideal form may at times be compromised *temporarily* in the interest of attaining the right results. However, under no circumstances should the altered form signal a violation of classical principles that promote the ideal goals.

During daily riding, strategies might be altered and form might deviate from the ideal temporarily. Yet this should never be regarded as a license that all means can be used to attain a goal. The means to our goals must always honor the horse by our respect for him and love for his individual virtues. The training methods should always promote calm, straight, supple and contented horses.

Riders will not know more than what their horses teach them. Coaching words mean nothing unless they cause behavior modification in the rider, and consequently, in the horse. The rider's subjective experience, through behavior modification, will teach him something. The more intelligence and feeling the rider possesses, the greater his subjective insights will be. In horsemanship words do not educate, only feelings do. Riders fortunate enough to ride many horses, including perhaps good movers and well-trained ones, will have a greater depth of feeling and a greater range of subjective experience than those, less fortunate, who are on a meager diet of one hobby horse.

The rider's education, both by coaching and by feeling the horse, is enhanced by insight. Riders diagnosed as having "no talent" often lack insight. They certainly show weakness in co-ordination and sense of rhythm. Though with hard work, those deficiencies can be compensated for. Where talent is lacking, industry and skills can substitute. Still, insight is the key to equestrian progress because it depends on the perceptions of the horse and the human ability to read them accurately.

Three

Coordinate Systems for Upgrading Dressage Instruction

The rapid growth of interest in dressage riding is a heart-warming world-wide phenomenon. This necessarily invites those only more-or-less prepared to teach classical equitation to fill the gap between excessive demand for instruction and a shrinking of an already meager supply of experts. Of course, any knowledgeable eye of a considerate and intelligent observer on the ground is better help than none to a rider in the saddle. Anyone a little ahead of another in riding experience or knowledge can be of assistance and useful as a teacher or helper of sorts, provided, of course, that with such an instructor no pretensions are made as to the possession of greater knowledge than is actually available. Little help is better than none. For riding is a sport of skills and an art of scholastic depth that cannot progress without the assistance of an observer. One should be on guard against advice received or advice given beyond the knowledge and the expertise of those who offer it.

There are basically two kinds of riders and they may be equally serious about their art. One is the rider-consumer who wishes to participate in the equestrian arts for the fulfillment of his/her and the horse's potentialities. The other is the career equestrian who may have the desire to become an expert and who can pass on his/her knowledge to both riders and horses. These people aspire to be the future coaches (of people) and trainers (of horses) who will absorb the knowledge of centuries past, to be passed on by them, uncorrupted, to generations of the future.

Here I want to warn that riding cannot be done by following a recipe book. It cannot be mechanized and done according to principles valid for technology. Riding will always need, ideally, daily observation by and help from another who is not in the saddle. Riding cannot be done with book in hand, following step-by-step instructions about how to do it. Yet, as in all sciences and arts, riding first has to be understood before it can successfully be practiced. Therefore I propose to do the useful deed of presenting here some "coordinate systems," some "orientational mental grids," along which instructional strategies can be mapped, and thus provide some basis for knowledgeable discussion among the young or aspiring generation of future instructors and trainers.

An instructor's goal should be to improve any horse under gymnastic training. In order to do so, he has to work through the more-or-less efficient intermediary, the rider. The instructor's paramount goal should always be to create an efficient, and with improvements, an effective rider who can be the right instrument for inducing correct development in the horse. Such a rider needs to know not only how to sit correctly but also how to influence the horse properly. Beyond these not so simple, yet minimal, requirements, each rider should master the theory of gymnastic training: to know what exercises to use as tools for development and how to use them in a gymnastically logical manner.

Riders have two "tool kits" with which to improve a horse and foster the unfolding of his gymnastic development. One of these is the rider's aiding system—the personal influences and tactually induced messages that the horse learns to correctly decode and respond to properly. The other tool kit consists of the gymnastically meaningful patterns riders use to train their horses. These patterns are central to this book. For without their proper utilization, no horse can progress toward the goals of the classical tradition in equitation. The patterns of the manege, the lines on which we move our horses, contribute to their gymnastic development more than what the rider's aids alone can contribute. Patterns allow performance that the rider, without them, could not cajole. Patterns have an added significance: By knowledgeable employment of them and by proper combination of them, they constitute the "tools" for rehabilitation, therapy and, finally, the hard-won gymnastic advancement. The proper training of riders should always include an insistence on teaching them the appropriate patterns to be used for the appropriate goals. Riding theory, without a thorough grasp of the usefulness of each pattern, would be void of meaning. Since the systematic schooling of riders is seldom available, the explanation of patterns and their usefulness now becomes the task for, and the purpose of, this book.

The proper training of the rider should precede any excessive attempts to train the horse. Do not attempt to advance a horse faster than the rider's abilities and skills warrant. For "progress" ill-gotten by a crooked, unbalanced, tense and disturbing rider constitutes negative learning for the horse.

Sometimes a horse is badgered by a frustrated rider at the proddings of an ambitious coach to do things he cannot because the rider is not skilled enough to communicate correctly. First and foremost the rider has to be created both academically and physically (as an athlete) before a coach can have proper access to the horse through the rider.

During instruction, regardless of the rider's level of preparedness, the coach must constantly cater to the needs of both horse and rider. The emphasis, however, must remain on the rider, especially until he reaches a level of effectiveness that allows him to become a "trainer of the horse." The coach's functions are divided between attention to the rider and to the horse. Coaching should address two consecutive categories: first diagnostic, and then curative. Two logical categories of work will follow: first determining the hierarchical importance of the problems and then knowing which problems are basic and cause the other, lesser ones. The curative remedies of the diagnosed problems have their hierarchy as well. Some remedies work more effectively or faster than others, and a coach should know how to differentiate and choose appropriately among them. This is the kernel of the coaching effort: knowing the appropriate remedies for the diagnosed problems!

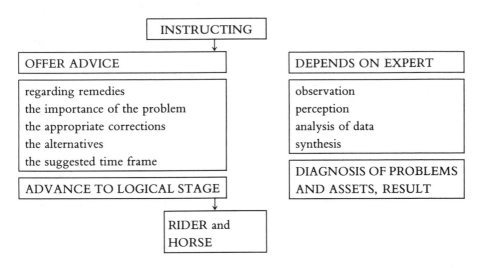

The diagnostic process emanates primarily from the horse. He "tells on his rider" and reveals all about his current condition. This is why during competition the judge uses only the horse's activities as guidelines for evaluating his progress and "pretends to ignore" the rider's destructive activities. However, remedying processes must begin with adjustments to the rider, who is the usual source of problems and shortcomings. The corrected rider's actions are transmitted to the horse where improved results will prove that the coaching was correct.

A coach's expertise increases with his ability to diagnose accurately, list the problems in order of importance and severity and offer the most effective means to remedy these problems. Insufficiencies in coaching, or for that matter training, are always due to wrong perception (diagnosis) and/or mistaken, inadequate and inappropriate remedies.

As an example of correct diagnosing, one could propose that relaxation and flexion of the horse's topline should precede concerns about lightening his forehand. Obviously, any expert knows that one cannot aspire to lighten the horse's forehand, which results from increased collection, without the horse first being properly stretched through his topline and working supplely through both his musculature and joints.

Two extremely important concepts relevant to horsemanship are power and freedom. Let me define them for purposes of discussion here. *Power* is the ability "to manipulate" one's external and internal environment and thus produce changes favorable to the "manipulator," i.e., the person of power. It follows, then, that only by exercising power can we induce desirable changes in the rider and his horse. The greater the ability of the rider to master his horse, the greater his chance of succeeding in the production of desirable changes. *Freedom* may be as extensive or as limited as is one's own awareness of the available choices. Thus, the rider becomes liberated by knowledge, both theoretically and experimentally. For knowledge increases awareness and lends itself to exploring a greater number of possible choices! Whether the issue is of diagnosis or of appropriate help (remedies), an awareness of choices and of "tools" available is essential to equestrian progress. Presuming that you accept my above-mentioned definitions of power and freedom, you may agree with me that *with freedom, power increases.* Conversely, with the diminishing of either, the other will proportionately decrease.

Instructors should consider yet another "coordinate system" by which to organize instructional strategies. As a coach, one must find one's position dynamically (ever-changingly) suspended among the seeming contradictions of the following ingredients of horsemanship:

Unique solutions suitable for specific needs that seldom arise.	versus	Commonly shared experiences remedied by generally accepted routine solution.
Individualized, highly specific horse and rider solution.	versus	Standardized and traditional means to problem-solving.
Varied patterning and frequent changes of activities.	versus	Prolonged, consistent, repetitive and enduring activities.
Creative approach and novel inventive strategies or patterns.	versus	Insistence of adherence to originally charted goals and programs that will achieve them.

Expert coaching will demonstrate the ease with which a teacher or rider can choose between seemingly opposing principles. A highly individualized approach will only be used when standard remedies have been tried and failed and only something novel will solve the problem. However, a good coach will know standard traditional procedures and exhaust their training possibilities before asking for a rare solution.

It is also important for a coach to know how much remedy each problem will need. The amount of corrective training action that can help a horse in restorative, therapeutic or athletic work is quite specific. Overdoing something can, on the other hand, be very harmful.

Similarly, one finds that in good coaching one must recommend seemingly opposite activities and emphasize seemingly opposing concepts. The greatness of the coach depends on his knowing the right time and circumstance to recommend the appropriate schooling activity. Examples of such seemingly opposite activities are these commonly known ones: Recommending an aggressive, insistent attitude toward the horse versus considering revisiting more fundamental demands, reviewing the comfortable known ways of the past. Another example would be the frequent initiation of new activities, promoting change (transitions or differing lengths of strides) versus harmonizing with whatever the horse offers and consolidating whatever the horse grants easily.

All these strategic attitudes have their legitimate place in daily training. The key to success is to find the most appropriate attitudes (means) at the most appropriate moment of need.

In good coaching and teaching one should be aware of the following philosophical possibilities for virtue:

1. The rider and the coach should often do what the horse enjoys doing but they should also learn to like what must be done. Thus, the virtuous rider knows both the pleasures of harmonizing with the best of the horse's achievements and repeating successful lessons that give both his horse and himself pleasure. But the rider must also learn of the pleasure that comes from a decreased threshold of pain. The virtue of greater endurance for what must be endured.

2. One should learn all the available traditional knowledge of horsemanship and adhere to its message respectfully. Yet one must also supplement that with one's own "intrinsic" knowledge, usually manifested in feelings. Often nonacademic but rather a priori (before the fact) knowledge is needed for the quickest decisions when riding.

3. One should ride for the moment the best one can. In other words, one should demand from the horse and from oneself the maximum possible output (performance) each moment, both in matters of content and style. This is fundamental for the formation of appropriate habits and making correct work the standard, not the exception. However, one may make appropriate compromises if not in content, temporarily in style, or by the reduction of pressures for high standards if it is in the interest of the future. That is, one should avoid the mistake of "painting over" a problem to make it look momentarily good. Instead, one should keep in mind that each moment of training addresses the entire future of the horse and is not just the immediate present.

4. One should ride with optimism, although some moments of pessimism and anxiety can spur the rider on to greater efforts. The joke "The optimist believes that he lives in the best of all possible worlds, and the pessimist knows that he does" reminds us that both attitudes have a constructive role in the development of the horse and rider. Without optimism for progress and contentment in whatever has been accomplished, riding would be masochistic. Without the pessimism to spur one on to greater perfection, progress would be slower.

5. Both variety and repetition of activities must be given appropriate roles. One ought to vary exercises and patterns. One ought to alter goals and strategies. Yet one must also know to pursue difficult things tenaciously, through repetition. Exactitude and habits, both extremely important in training, are born of repetition!

6. Finally, one's horsemanship should entail goals that are *macrocosmic*, that is, contributing to the art of riding with enduring validity and dignity. But horsemanship should also remain *microcosmic*, to be personally satisfactory, fulfilling,

rewarding in a very intimate, private sense. This makes riding relevant to one's own life experience. Thus, a fine equestrian should aspire to be historically noteworthy, an example to emulate, a source of inspiration for perfection. Yet, he should also continue interacting with his innermost self and become a finer human being in a profound, and permanent, way.

Four

Training Traditions: Sharing the Arena

Riding, for centuries, was done by many riders sharing one arena, whether they were riding under instruction or training without advice. In sharp contrast to this tradition, we see that in the Anglo-Saxon countries coaching dressage relies mostly on the individual lesson. The rider, when not being coached, often does his usual daily schooling alone as well. Most of the riders that I teach or judge, work their horses alone in an arena, which is usually only the size of a dressage competition arena or smaller. This isolation and confinement of horse and rider creates unusual training and schooling conditions. Some of them may be beneficial but most are detrimental to progress.

The advantages of riding alone and of receiving individual instruction are well known and are now widely favored. While jumping and cross-country riding enthusiasts also often work alone, they share arenas when they are under instruction. Jumping coaching is frequently done in group work.

The advantages of riding in groups and taking group lessons are numerous, for example, scattering the riders in the available space and allowing them to work individually on their own problems and administer to their horse's unique needs. Alternately, riders can be required to move in a "class formation"

20

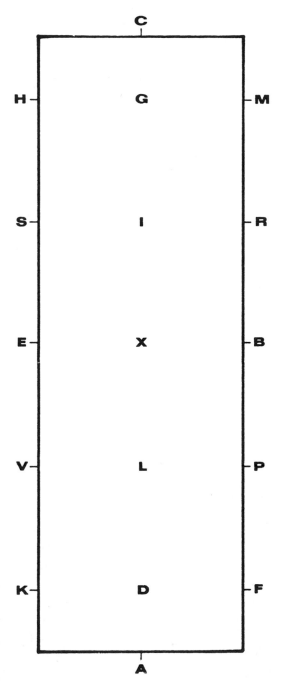

This is the standard dressage arena. All international competitions, including Olympic Games and World Championships, are held in such an arena, and many riders train in one daily.

Its dimensions are 60m (198 ft.) long by 20m (66 ft.) wide. The corner letters, such as M, are placed 6m (19' 10") from the nearest corner of the arena. The distances between the letters along the long wall, such as the distance from M to R, measure 12m (39' 7"). Horses must always enter and exit at A, and for this reason a 2m (6' 6") segment of the short wall in front of A is removed or kept open.

The points of the arena that are important for exact patterning are marked with letters. There are also letters at points lined up along the center line of the arena, always where they represent the halfway point between letters on opposite walls. For example, G designates the halfway point between M and H. These letters and their location are memorized by most riders and certainly by all who compete. Competition tests are written by designating each pattern with the help of letters. Even during training, coaches call for exercises by designating the patterns by letters.

No one knows for sure, in spite of considerable research, why these letters are placed at these locations. There seems to be no logic to it. Those of us who ride and teach in this standard manege have long since stopped worrying about its history and respect it as part of the mystique of any great tradition.

under command, which both prescribes for them the patterns and calls for common tasks to be performed in unison. These group formations might work along the rail, either with the riders evenly distributed or with them following a lead rider while they maintain a distance of two lengths apart. Of course, this is for reasons of safety and privacy as well as maneuverability over the patterns. Most riding in the past, including in the famous riding academies and institutions, was done in such a manner.

Horses are highly social animals that live in herds in their natural state, and they need and like each other. This is why good stables offer horses a view of each other in their boxes. Horses soon behave abnormally when isolated from others and become neurotic backyard pets. Often, upon seeing another horse, they break out in the kind of disturbed whinnying that is more akin to screaming. Equally neurotic behavior is the exaggerated dodging and ducking of other horses approaching in the arena or warm-up ring. Other times, isolated horses might turn to aggression rather than shyness and lash out, kick or bite at others. Pinning their ears and tensing their nostrils, they express mistrust toward other horses. Horses must accept each other, and those who share competition arenas know that.

Great benefits may be gained by riders who work in the company of others. Some of the best learning, the finest insights, can come about by observing others riding. Especially when riders sharing a space are like-minded companions, the way they really should be. For while horses are herd animals, their riders should also constitute an equestrian community. Even observing bad riders who follow disagreeable training philosophies can help make clear all the many things one ought not to do. Indeed, the observation of bad riders may fill one with gladness for one's commitment to the right scholarship, the right ways through kindness and reward.

Riders who work in groups will inevitably enrich their equestrian experience, for they can simultaneously feel subjective input from their horse, while observing objectively the experiences others have with their horses. In a way, one rides in one's mind all horses one observes under training. When I coach riders, I habitually "ride along" with them in both a physical and emotional sense.

There is no way one can ever acquire complete equestrian knowledge. Every horse is vastly different and also reacts differently from one moment to the next. The horse's state of mind, indeed, fluctuates between the "instinctively coded" behavior of the pasture and the learned, conditioned behavior induced by the partnership and culture of the rider. The horse's depth of concentration varies highly and remains always dependent on his nature, his level of training, submission to the rider and the current stimuli in the area. Each rider's knowledge will also be enhanced by discussing training matters with other riders.

Learning also takes place when it is not based on formal, structured instruction. Often, learning is informal and as if by osmosis. Learning is confirmed only when it is internalized and becomes subjective by being rider-specific. This is knowing by experiencing. There is a great difference between believing in what an instructor says or knowing it by the validation of first-hand experience. The knowing of riding is much helped by being in and riding in the company of others.

In the Spanish Riding School riders work together in groups. They perform in groups, both in precise formation and as individuals. Similarly, schooling in the famous stallion centers of the Hanoverian and Wesphalian horses, we see daily group work. They also show their stallions and parade them in groups. In all of these institutions professionalism, expertise and thorough knowledge of the classical tradition of horsemanship determine the direction of the training programs. Schooling in groups remains, by choice and by wisdom. The result is excellence shown by quiet, concentrating, obedient stallions. In fact, most often the best horsemanship is seen when riders share an arena, rather than in competition when one rider is viewed by five judges.

Individual instruction is often necessary. However, it is not always the best way to utilize the knowledge and resources of a coach. Comments made by an instructor to any rider could be beneficial to others within earshot. All good coaching commentary is relevant, one way or another, to the others in the area even though they are not addressed directly. Riders in a group can concentrate on feelings received from the horse because the instructor's comments do not always target the same rider. In fact, some individual instruction can be so crowded with speech and ideas that the rider has neither time nor energy left for focusing on the horse. A sensitive instructor will often adjust both the quantity and the quality of verbalization in recognition of the individual needs of each rider for a balance between instructional noise and fruitful silence.

The art of riding consists of many general principles that can best be explained to groups rather than wastefully repeated to individuals. The principles of schooling horses, the philosophy (ethics) of training and the logical procedures can be well taught to groups. Most importantly, however, and this is at the heart of this book's subject matter, the meaning and usefulness of patterns can best be taught to groups moving over them in unison. Riders train their horses with two sets of training "tools." One tool is their personal influence of the horse's balance, rhythm and energy output by their behavior in the saddle. The other tool encompasses all the logical and proper patterns of the manege and their combinations. The infinite variety of patterns combine into near-infinite possibilities for improving the horse whatever his therapeutic or gymnastic needs may be.

Individualized instruction, however, is highly valuable for three specific purposes.

1. For correcting persistent and severe faults. These must be identified and their correction monitored.
2. For polishing to perfection the efforts achieved in group situations. The finishing touches to competition movements and the strategies suitable to specific horse-and-rider team needs are based on highly individualized suggestions and personalized insights.
3. Individualized instruction to beginners is absolutely indispensable. They need constant monitoring and advice. They lack the proper controls when left to their own devices. These beginners must often be lunged until they develop a balanced, deep, independent seat by which they can earn the jcontrol of their horse and the holding of their reins.

After a properly founded seat is achieved, the rider will have earned his right to control his horse unattended by a constant monitor. Therefore he will arrive at a stage of development based on diversification. He will have earned his place among others, indeed as a member of a group.

Proper behavior while riding in a group, whether under instruction or not, is very important. The basic ingredients of proper group behavior are based on a constant attention to the safety and needs of others sharing the area. The very definition of good manners is a constant concern for the needs of others. Such a concern, or familiarity with propriety and politeness, can lead any rider to a logical list of guiding principles for their behavior while riding in a group. The few I will list here are not all-inclusive. They are helpful guidelines.

RULES TO BE OBSERVED WHEN RIDING IN A GROUP

Riders in a group should ride in such a way as not to disturb others and make the shared area safe for them all. While being aware of the needs of others, be alert for your own safety as well. Be aware of the position as well as the intended direction of all other riders and put yourself into a space that promotes mutual safety.

- When riding in a class keep a minimum of one length away from the horse ahead of you and expect the same safe distance to be kept by the rider following you.
- Whatever you do, including standing to hear instruction, keep your horse away from all others at a distance safe enough from kicking.
- When seeking correct distribution (by repositioning yourself), you may cross through the arena, circle to find an appropriate opening for yourself. Never ever pass another horse parallel with it, in racing fashion (or like automobiles).
- Do not cross the logical and anticipated path of progression of another horse.
- Stop your horse and stand still when another rider is in trouble, i.e., has fallen off or is dealing with his horse rearing or running away or bucking, etc.
- If working scattered throughout the arena rather than in unison as a class, make sure that slow-moving horses work

close to the center of the arena while faster-moving ones are nearer the rails, i.e., cantering should be by the rail while walking is toward the center.

- Pass oncoming horses as you would pass an oncoming car while driving. Stay to the right side of the path, allowing left hands to meet.
- When working as a class, the lead horse must allow the end of the class to trail along the rail and complete the pattern inward, away from the rail. For example, when changing rein on the diagonal, upon arrival in the corner and encountering the remaining horses of the class still progressing there, the lead horse must avoid crossing their paths, allowing them to use the rail and taking an inner path until the vacant rail allows returning to it.
- When approaching cavalletti poles, jumps or obstacles, keep enough distance from other horses to enable you to turn your horse away on an arc if the unit should be disturbed by any horse ahead of yours. Do not avoid a disturbed obstacle by stopping but by riding an acceptable half–circle away from it, which allows the rest of the riders to progress without losing rhythm or balance. Return to an available space in the class and await your turn to approach the obstacle again. Never just "butt in" to compensate for your earlier inability to jump. Do not take your horse over any obstacle that has been disturbed.
- If you need to adjust any equipment, you must vacate the path of others by going to the center of the arena where you must halt to make the adjustments, e.g., changing the length of the stirrups, tightening the girth or removing spurs.
- When anyone is advised, corrected or instructed in the arena, you must also make the relevant adjustments and improvements. When instructing a group of riders, the instructor customarily mentions a shortcoming by naming the rider who shows the fault most. However, you must assume that you need the same adjustment or correction and take care of it as if the instructor spoke to you directly by name.
- Show humility by always doing your best without expecting special indulgence from your instructor.

Five

The Patterns of
the Manege

Various patterns are ridden, usually, to practice required movements in competitions. This is like putting the cart before the horse. Competition patterns are none other than the often-ridden training patterns used by judges as tools for evaluating the gymnastic development of the athletic horse. Riders should not practice patterns merely because they will have to ride them in competition tests. Instead, they should know the gymnastic usefulness and the developmental purpose invested in each. One must realize that there are a great many more useful patterns than those used as evaluative instruments in standardized dressage tests. In fact, the newly popular "freestyle" classes offer the imaginative rider the possibility of creating and using novel patterns and avoiding the repetition of those used in standard tests. Innovative patterns are not only welcome compositional features in a freestyle test, but can help earn higher scores on originality and artistic merit. However, care must be taken that the patterns used either for training or in freestyle competition should remain within the acceptable realm of classical development. For neither a knowledgeable competition judge nor a tormented horse would reward a rider who contrived useless, illogical and unacceptable patterns just for the sake of novelty. As in all art, in the art of riding there are boundaries to the liberties that artists may take in expression.

In Chapter 4 I explained that riders have two "tools" for the gymnastic improvement of their horses. I would like to emphasize that by using the term "tools" in no way means to imply that riding is mechanical or can be approached through technology. In fact, most of the grave misunderstandings in horsemanship can be blamed on mechanizing riding into a technology! Even mechanically programmed horses are a repulsive reminder of how many riders fall victim to the cultural understanding about a "rational, mechanical universe." All things obeying push buttons, switches and levers are adored examples of the technological slave that comforts its human controller. The horse is not a machine! Horsemanship is not a technology!

Riders who use their two tool kits, or training means, do so to influence the horse's understanding of what they wish of him. Riders with enough academic expertise and practical riding skills will explore and then develop the horse's potentialities according to a scientifically understood system. One of the rider's tool kits is his aiding system, that is, personally influencing and controlling the horse by tactual communication. Such communication falls into two conceptually different categories. On the one hand, riders seek absolute harmony in partnership with the horse, and that is achieved when the rider approves (and rewards) the status quo, the horse's offering. On the other hand, the rider can willfully disturb the perfect harmony to make something different happen. Still within the means of partnership (rather than antagonism), the rider more or less disturbs the status quo and guides his horse toward a new achievement. All of this is done by the rider tactually (weight, balance, pressure points, etc.) influencing the horse's flexion, elasticity, suppleness, balance, rhythm, impulsion and engagement. These rider-initiated messages must be taught to the horse clearly, much as a foreign language is taught to us. We must know and the horse must know, the exact meaning of each tactual stimulus of the rider. Precision of communication by the rider, and the horse's understanding of it, develop gradually and its result is obedience.

The more refinement and subtleties that rider communications include, the greater the contents of this tool kit are for his use. Hypothetically, as an ideal, one could imagine a riding master having such an extensive and precise system of refined aids, and such lucid communication qualities, that he would never need a "second tool kit" for advancing his horse. He would then be able to develop all his horse's potentialities by riding him on a straight path from here to there, without ever using any patterns.

Hence we always need our "second tool kit," which contains the various patterns one can travel on in a manege. There are many possible patterns, and they can combine into a potentially infinite number—just as combinations of numbers can create telephone books. It is the rider's obligation to learn the patterns that have proven particularly useful in the gymnastic development of most horses most of the time throughout the long history of academic equitation. Riders should pursue the scholarship of knowing how various exercises and patterns influence the various parts of the horse's anatomy.

Patterns should not be used randomly or ignorantly, because in horsemanship there is no neutrality. You are either furthering the horse's well-being or destroying it. You either "make or break" your horse but you are never in a "holding pattern" where you can think to yourself, How should we just muddle through with this? The rider should also have an understanding of how these patterns help in restorative, rehabilitative and gymnastic work. Depending on the way and the extent to which patterns are used, they can be "medicinal" or corrective or developmental! As if this task were not already overwhelming, I must also remind riders that patterns, not being "mechanical," have no magical effects on the horse. Rather by riding an appropriate variety of them, one contributes to the total development of the entire horse. Much as the rider should not think "to aid" but rather feel always as an "aiding system" that works as if all of him is there, so should the horse be regarded as one, wholesome, living organism. Riders who work on the horse "in bits and pieces" will ride their horses asunder, rather than into a united edifice. It reminds us, once again, of the relevance of the Gestalt theory of reality: a view of reality that proposes that everything is more than the sum of its composite parts. For it is in the arrangements (configuration equals Gestalt) of the constituent parts that the edifice is finally determined.

Each pattern, therefore, develops the entire horse. Yet each one will also specifically help in the strengthening, stretching, suppling, softening, swinging or articulating of some muscle or joint. They will benefit specifically certain muscular movements or skeletal efficiency.

Similarly, when evaluating a horse's progress through competition patterns, judges must know the "primary purpose" of each pattern—that is, the reason for their being required. But judges must also "computerize" the information they receive from their overall impression that emerges from the "general impressions" revealed consistently through all the movements performed.

Whenever possible, the rider's obligation is to use his influences to achieve the gymnastic goals. In short, extensions, collections, bending, two-track movements, should rely on the rider's equitational skills for perfection. However, when these skills are insufficient the rider should turn to the use of proper patterns for assistance. Ideally, riders should have as large a "pattern vocabulary" as possible. In this book I wish to assist in achieving that.

Far from moving about at random in the arena, patterns were developed as logical solutions to problems. The most commonly used pattern is called "going large," which is the following of the fence line at the perimeter of the manege. This is far from being the easiest of patterns and yet most riders consider it a basic staple and the "simple thing" to use even for warming up. In fact, progression along the straight walls with a truly straightened horse, after bending him evenly in every one of the corners, is one of the most difficult tasks to achieve. Yet often for the lack of a better idea, riders will just "hug the fence" and go round and round the available space.

Longitudinal flexion, connecting the energies of the haunches through an elevated, flexed and stretched spine, can be best developed by performing "mini-transitions," called half-halts. They can also be developed, of course, by performing major transitions from one gait to another. However, the suppling and therefore strengthening of the joints can best be accomplished by lateral work. The lateral bending of the horse's spine, and therefore torso, provides "shock absorption" on curving patterns. Because a bending horse must use each hind leg dissimilarly, one hind leg will stress certain joints differently than the other, and while this provides shock absorption while impacting the ground, it also causes development in the joints used with most articulation. Consequently, moving on arcs will strengthen and elasticize the horse's joints. Without such strengthening, all suppling, collection and engagement would be impossible.

While every pattern contributes interchangeably and in an overlapping fashion to the total development of the entire horse, specific patterns tend to correct specific problems, administer to specific needs and improve specific developmental phases. In this book, when discussing patterns and "figures," I will suggest their specific benefits and their logical and reasonable employment in the interest of the horse.

The rider asks, influences, instructs and controls. Patterns can develop the horse's physique but cannot train him. Only a rider can train a horse. While this book is dedicated to the explanation of patterns and their various uses, one must, in this chapter, briefly recall certain indispensable principles of equitation. For ultimately, even patterns fail to help if the rider's influences are wrong.

Horses are primarily schooled by the rider's influences and only assisted by the developmental virtues of patterns.

HALF-HALTS AND THEIR RELATIONSHIP TO COLLECTION

Half-halts facilitate the readjusting of the horse's balance. You execute one any time you need to rebalance the horse, usually to increase his collection. Since the only correct definition of collection is an increase in weight-bearing by the haunches, the definition of half-halt is an action that produces this effect. A half-halt must precede all transitions and every change from traveling straight to traveling bent. Each time you bend a horse or straighten him after bending, you must perform a half-halt.

It is the activity that appears most frequently when you ride.

The half-halt consists of two things. The first is a restraint of the forehand, to make it wait until the hind end can reach toward it and reconnect the hocks to the muzzle. This is the restrictive part of the action and it begs the horse not to progress in space quite as much as it did earlier. The second phase of the activity allows the haunches to come through; that is, it opens the gates of progression to continue onward. The combination of these two actions must be without hesitation and without any loss of rhythm. Both the restraining and the driving through must flow through the identical rhythmic profile.

The human who executes the half-halt must produce it in himself. The upper half of the rider's body is the restrictor that produces a passive resistance. The torso tucks the pelvis more forward with the abdominal muscles; the shoulder blades must be flat to fold the shoulders back and down, thereby elevating the ribcage and sending it ahead of the upper arms. The elbows point downward from perpendicular upper arms, which feel as if part and parcel of a "monolithic torso." Such arms can produce a passive—rather than harmfully active—resistance. One must overcome any temptation to follow, jar, quiver or yield involuntarily because of ill-placed shoulders, upper arms, elbows and the "cabinetry" of the ribcage. The straight back and vertical upper arm, with elbows perpendicular to the ground, must form a "plumb line." Your upper body (cabinetry) must remain isometrically silent in order to convey to the horse that he must slow the progression of his forehand. The lower part of the torso simultaneously drives. You must feel split at the waistline. The upper body sustains a passive resistance, and that increases the pressure of your body weight on the horse, which combined with the increase in the muscle tone lends the lower body greater driving power. The lumbar back, the pelvic pressure and the legs combine into a driving force. The same isometric unity that produces the "whoa" with the upper body simultaneously lends effectiveness to the driving apparatus of the lower body and the legs.

Half-halts are not executed with the hands. The hands holding the reins correctly must become extensions of the activities and position of the torso and the seat. Hands must not "check" the bit, which is a polite expression for chucking a horse in the teeth. Hands must not "squeeze" on the bit, which is polite language for pulling. Whatever restraints hands must or ought to deliver must come from the rider's seat as his torso increases the weight effectiveness downward-forward on the horse's back. One "sinks down" to restrain the forehand. Horses do not perceive the rider's "seat" where he sits or at his pelvis and buttocks. Horses perceive the seat at the rider's elbows! Correctly placed and steadily held, elbows transfer the positional and muscular pressures of the torso correctly and instantly to the bit. The horse's mouth feels the seat from the elbows. During half-halts the perpetual driving with legs and seat remains important. The horse must be allowed to shape his neck; the rider must never shorten, hoist or confine it.

The half-halt may start with a moment's stress in the rider's structure, a passive resistance to the horse's progression in space. However, that sensation must be followed by one of great fluency and liquidity. When the horse steps through, he hikes his back and becomes a "taller hoop." His neck feels more liquid as it hangs from the top muscle's flexion, with the head hanging supply as if a chandelier from the ceiling. The result is increased engagement and suppleness.

The second phase of every half-halt is a period of confirmation and approval. You have to go with what the horse has given you for a while. The only way to instruct a horse is to tell him when he is right, and the minimal expression of approval is harmony. Therefore the half-halt is followed by a period of synchronization, which produces total harmony. This "oneness" is a dancing partnership because it is unity with rhythm. This ideal partnering should be maintained until the next half-halt is necessitated.

Remember that half-halts should never be mechanical. Nothing in riding should be mechanical because riding is, in many ways, the opposite of technology! Each half-halt done is different from all the others. The period of restraint (passive resistance) exchanged for a period of forward flow always differs. How long you sustain each, how the proportion of restraint to drive is worked out and how much lightness of forehand, engagement of haunches may be produced, will vary. But even if no two half-halts are identical, they always emphasize the change in the balance of the horse for the better. If you do not feel improvement in the balance, then you have not succeeded in performing a half-halt.

DEVELOPING COLLECTION

All energies that cause the correct posture of the horse and supplies all his transportation originate in the haunches. Collection refers to any activity that increases the assumption of weight by the horse's hindquarters. Collection, therefore, is a relative condition. Either more or less of it can be produced. Seldom sustained in its maximum form, collection is a process that cannot be thought of as being terminated, frozen, achieved, monumentalized or arrived at. However, collection can refer to a specific standard of behavior that denotes a greatly increased weight assumption by the hindquarters. This shifting of the horse's center of gravity toward the haunches liberates his forehand from unnecessary weight and saves it from stress. The forelegs being the weaker, riders learned early the value of saving them and conserving their health.

Collection is among the several possible synonyms for classical gymnastic riding. Classical equitation always seeks to promote the assumption of more weight by the haunches, through any and all of its frequently practiced exercises. Collection, as everything in correct training, is achieved or increased gradually and progressively, and only when work is based on thorough knowledge. The means to collection are many, and not all involve actual "acts of collecting." Therefore, only knowledgeable riders will practice the relevant means for producing collection.

Elements of collection include the following observable features:

1. The horse increases his pelvic tuck by tilting his hips forward by a rounding and tucking of his lumbar region.
2. The lumbar area increases its flexion, becomes stretched and moves with increased articulation.

3. The hind legs move more forward under the center of gravity.

4. The joints in the hind legs articulate more so as to lift higher.

The last two effects, which influence the placing of the hind legs, depend on the degree to which the horse is capable of a lumbar tucking, which allows the pelvis to tilt forward and under. In this sense collection gains a more proper conceptual dimension. For with the lumbar and pelvic activities of collection one can produce the most impressive extended trot, which sinks down behind and floats onward and upward in slow motion as if mounting a staircase two steps at a time.

Collection increases the strength of the haunches, and as that strength becomes available, it in turn opens the possibility for further, more intense, collection. Collection always results in increased flexibility, and therefore strength, in the joints. Increased elasticity in the muscles can propel the skeleton with more precise strides. As the haunches strengthen, they assume more of the weight, shift the center of gravity toward them and liberate the forehand. Posture becomes taller, and the carriage becomes more graceful.

Collection is facilitated, in particular, by exercises on smaller patterns, by doing transitions both within the gaits (extension and collection) and from one gait to another, and by riding on two tracks. Collection results in the lowering of the croup (lumbar tucking) and the elevation of the withers (bouncing the withers higher when moving), which observers discern as a "sitting" horse with a "liberated" forehand. It encourages the ideal of a horse who need not dwell but merely pass over his forehand while moving. This reinforces the concept that ultimately all exercises that succeed in roundness (the stretched and pushed-up spine) of the horse's topline, flexion (articulation) in his joints and elevation of the forehand into a taller posture (carriage) are collection exercises.

Collection can succeed only if the rider can maintain, or even increase, energy (activity) of the haunches while actually slowing his progress through space. The ability to turn energy into better posture rather than more rapid transportation is essential to collection! To be able to elevate the strides, and thus shorten them, is vastly important. Collection cadences the horse, "dances him up" with minimum, precise impaction on the ground, resulting in maximum floatation and suspension. Collection is the greatest proof of the rider's ability to use the energy he inspires in his horse for a better body position and carriage, thereby discouraging evasion by speed. Let us remember that speed and crookedness are the only two evasions of the horse as he resists the rider's desire to gain control over (submission of) the haunches!

Collection is transportation born of the finest carriage: haunches tucked under, elevated strides, slow (majestic) rhythm, cadenced definition of the gaits. All these result in great activity in the haunches with a smoothness of motion that suggests tranquillity and effortlessness in progression. Haste is the enemy of collection! So is inactivity in the haunches. Collection is tested and verified best by performing a rein-back (unfortunately a misnomer), the pirouettes in both walk and canter and the trot-like piaffe and passage. Collection must also be tested and verified through the so-called extreme transitions, such as going from halt to canter or from canter to halt, or generating a piaffe from the halt and terminating it at a halt.

THE HALT AS A TRAINING DEVICE

The halt may be referred to as "full halt" (as opposed to the half-halt) or as a "full parade," depending on the speaker or the writer. Halts, by any name, are very important in dressage training. Because of the gymnastic significance of halting, every competition dressage test has a minimum of two halts. In higher-level competition tests the number of halts requested increase and the transitions to them and from them become more demanding. Tests for competitions are merely evaluative devices for what training has done to improve the horse.

In the training of a dressage horse the importance of halts is magnified because frequent and good halts ensure collection. The skill, the strength and the ability to collect are greatly enhanced by correctly executed halts.

Collection, as noted before, is defined as the shifting of the center of gravity from the forehand toward the haunches. A properly executed halt represents a very high level of collection. The halt is not merely a result of inaction. It is not a sign of laziness or resistance to forward movement. Far from it. Halts collect because the center of gravity shifts toward the haunches whenever a horse moving at a certain speed (3 to 14 miles per hour, for instance) stops to produce a zero-miles-per-hour performance. The speed terminates, yet the horse must remain collected and filled with the energy that readies him to move onward and forward once again.

A correct halt is really a "movement," one in which the forward progression has temporarily been omitted. Yet the horse must remain ready for "transportation" while he is temporarily not in progression through space. The posture of the horse at the halt must suggest latent movement. Readiness to depart from the halt, immobility filled with the energy necessary to depart it, are the essential requirements of a good halt.

Two things define a good halt. The first is immobility. Usually less than 6 seconds of immobility is not sufficient to qualify for a good halt. If the horse moves after the halt, even if he tosses his head or fidgets or looks up and sideways, or does anything that is other than utter immobility, the halt is impaired. If a horse does not maintain immobility for at least 6 seconds, he may have merely paused, lost impulsion or resisted but did not halt. The second requirement for a good halt is perfection of balance. This is demonstrated by the squareness of the halt. If one were to use a scale to evaluate any halt, the worst kind would be one in which the horse stopped with all his legs separated (out of balance) and commenced to fidget. A little improvement would be shown if the hind legs stayed together with only the front ones separated. Much better is the kind of halt in which the front legs square and the hind ones are a little apart. But when a halt is good, all four feet stand square.

To perform a halt, one first prepares the horse with half-halts. A half-halt readjusts the horse's balance and begins the process of collection. After successfully rebalancing, one ceases to drive, and instead of yielding with the torso or hands to the harmonious motions of the horse, the torso, and its extension, the hands, sustain the passive resistance. While remaining balanced the rider uses his torso and the closure of the upper legs as "brakes" (i.e., increase of friction). In order to increase friction and convey to the horse restraint without inhibition to the haunches or confinement to the neck, the rider should round his lumbar back (lower back) with stronger abdominal muscle contraction. This action is analogous to one's lifting the back legs of a kitchen chair off the floor by bracing the abdomen, which pushes the pelvis forward relative to the retarding position of the shoulders. It is important that while pressing the pelvis downward and forward with the rounding lumbar region and the contracted abdomen, one must not tense the muscles of the buttocks or pinch with them. Nor should one brace against the stirrups but rather retain the correctly hanging, draped contact position of the legs. Closing the knees and contracting the muscles of the thighs help increase the friction, producing additional "braking" and also contribute to the rider's steadiness of balance.

Simply by omitting forward progression, replacing it with passive resistance (lack of following motions) and adding greater friction (the brakes) one can halt a horse without ever pulling or jerking the reins. When a horse is well-schooled, he will halt in balance and the rider will feel so relaxed that omission to propel the horse squared him into a halt.

A good halt is always performed handless. The reins merely transmit what the seat and torso have spoken. What the seat and legs say will travel out through the reins and arrive at the muzzle, but the hand should not make any separate gesture, effort or signal without the seat and legs. The most common rider error in halting is hand interference. Pulling on a horse's mouth and shortening his neck are mistakes for which the horse charges the toll of a bad halt. Stopping a horse by pulling backward with the hands will stop the horse on the forehand, and it will stiffen his neck and hollow his back. These are unacceptable faults that violate the requirements for suppleness, elasticity, balance and tranquillity.

It should be understood that perfect halts do not happen right away. One develops good halts gradually and by teaching the halt precisely, reviewing it consistently and often. Much like all gymnastic exercises, the halt is perfected by correcting it a little bit each time. Square the legs right from the beginning. Horses have excellent muscular memories and a fantastic sense of balance (by which they survive in nature!). Show repeatedly how a square halt feels right and in fact balances the horse into one of the positions in which he can take a nap. Horses do sleep standing up if they so wish! Overcorrecting a horse by unnecessarily adjusting him after he has halted, to insure squareness, leads to fidgety attitudes. Lack of immobility is a great fault.

Once a horse has learned to halt, he will do it within a few strides and eventually will halt even from a collected canter at the time you "think" halt. But such fine results come with time. As in all teaching, be patient and consistent, and repeat. Help your horse to understand your wish rather than force him to accept it. Always reward good efforts and halts well done. Confirm when things go right, clarify when they become muddled. Build the horse's skills and strengths through his attention and devotion to you. He will learn his exercises well and as fast as he can.

Six

Patterns as Training Strategies

THE GOALS OF TRAINING

The principal goals of training horses can be very simply stated. Prolonging the serviceable life of the horse and protecting his utilitarian value to the rider, coincide with the horse's need to live a life void of pain and stress. To achieve this simply stated but hard to attain objective, one must promote two developmental goals for the horse.

1. The horse should become able and competent in regaining his natural balance in the basic gaits of walk, trot and canter under the added weight of the rider and saddlery.
2. Having attained natural balance and purity of the gaits under the rider, we now propose to improve the natural gaits of the horse gradually. We do this by development (strength, elasticity and suppleness), which promotes the shifting of the center of gravity gradually toward the haunches (thereby liberating the more tender forehand) of the horse and by promoting cadencing. The latter refers to the horse's ability to travel under the foreign weight of the rider with greater

This is Flutewind, a purebred Trakehner gelding by Marduc. Nothing can be more beautiful than an unencumbered horse floating in trot. Here is everything the rider must seek to regain under the saddle and the rider's weight: the horse moving effortlessly in natural balance, with great suspension, elastic steps and totally relaxed. Furthermore, the horse is engaged enough to move voluntarily "uphill," and he is straight. He is, as he should be, stretched longitudinally and yet in that magic situation when all good things come together. The gait (trot) is magnified, it is cadenced, it is "uphill." It is engaged on the haunches. The forehand liberated, the neck and head in graceful carriage. A great calm presides over this tremendous expression of energy. The movement blankets the horse as he travels over territory in suspended flight. Gravity-defying, graceful, grand.

The rider can and ought to develop only the natural potentialities (gifts) of the horse. Here, by conformation, by elasticity of motion, a well-bred mind and great physical beauty, a great deal of potential is in reserve for the rider to develop. An example of "nature's gift" to be nurtured by the art of riding. Photo: Rebecca Whitcombe.

suspension, covering ground by flight over it. Cadencing is made possible by skills born of strength and suppleness that allow the horse a very precise and brief impaction on the ground (footfall) to produce a more (than naturally volunteered) elongated flotation over space—with minimum touch-down and effort, maximum transportation while airborne.

Both of these seemingly simple goals can be achieved only by systematic, gradual and knowledgeable work based on a daily recapitulation of a therapeutic, rehabilitative and athletic work program for the horse. While I discuss gymnastically meaningful patterns in this book, I will only find them useful in the light of these basic goals. No pattern is ever useful or scholastically logical unless it contributes to the development of the horse's natural gaits and to the unfolding of his inherited potentialities, and does it in such a way that it provides the horse with an enjoyable, painless working life.

A rider animated by love and respect for his horse will never submit him to exercises not invested with meaning. All patterns practiced in the manege have purpose and meaning. To decode, decipher, interpret and utilize them is my purpose.

TRAINING STRATEGIES

Here let me discuss some useful training strategies and the reasoning behind them.

- Dare to take a chance. Test carefully the parameters of your horse's willingness and ability to perform a certain movement or pattern. Often he will. When the horse is physically ready and mentally willing, he will give you a performance you were not sure you could get. Courage is the primary virtue (in life) in horsemanship. A rider who lacks the courage to take a chance will not succeed in unfolding his horse's potentialities. The vast reserves of the horse's capabilities are only given to the courageous rider. Horses have little tolerance for the timid and silently despise the reluctant by not giving them the performance that they could give, had it been honored by courage.
- Be opportunistic and take with gratitude the voluntary performance of your horse. Often when not asked, the horse will do something rather valuable, and if so, we should pretend that we wanted it. Be quick to reward useful activities you believe you have gotten "by mistake." A horse seldom makes a mistake! The rider often does. Poorly com-

municated, overzealously requested, confusingly aided movements often communicate to the horse something other than what the rider intended. The horse will perform not what the rider had in mind but rather what the rider physically directed. Horses will do almost anything for the rider but read his mind. What we hope to get, we must ask for with skill, clarity, consistency and precision. Failing to do so, our horse will act according to his perception of our instruction or request. When he does, pretend that you wanted what he is offering: Never admit to your horse that you made a mistake by punishing his action! Remaining in our horse's confidence is far more important than willfully asserting ourselves for the attainment of superficial, temporary goals. When we err, the horse will perform and we apologize by taking his performance as if that were our wish. A lesson in humility, the second most important equestrian virtue.

- Mine the treasures of the horse's anticipations. If we dare expect the horse to learn from our meager communications, we must presume that he learns much of what we ask for by monitoring consistency. Here a pressure, there a pressure and we hope to gain this or that. The horse learns to read our often-blurred language. Finally, when he is keen, he anticipates our wishes because we, often inadvertently, have given him a clue—a customary, preliminary clue we may not even be aware of. We must learn to be our horse's pupil, not just his teacher. This acceptance of being tutored by an intelligent horse is the third virtue of good horsemanship. Learn to listen and accept the performance the horse delivers in anticipation of your wish before the planned controls are implemented. Those riders who punish the horse for anticipating degrade his intelligence and punish his brilliance in detecting the rider's wish while it is still a hidden secret in the rider's mind. But to a sensitive horse, the rider gives away the secrets of his mind by letting his clumsy body speak about them before its time!

WORKING WITH THE UNGYMNASTICIZED HORSE

The daily work of a horse should be a capsulized effort of the long-term developmental needs of a horse. At the very beginning of gymnastic training a horse should not move on so-called patterns, but rather, ideally, be ridden outdoors or in areas large enough to give the illusion of being outdoors. A green horse must move forward on long lines, much like a road or crossing meadows. If turns are involved or the tracks are rather confiningly narrow or tightly follow a rail, the rider should be determined to compromise exactitude of patterns in the interest of following the horse's insecure balance. The most important concept at the beginning of training is to harmonize, unite, the center of gravity of the rider with that of the horse. Wherever the horse drifts as he attempts to balance under the foreign weight of the rider, there must the rider follow. Until the horse becomes strong enough to carry his rider and until he learns the skills of balancing his rider, the latter must help him by remaining exactly above the horse's center of gravity.

The untrained, green horse will be "staggering" under the rider and drifting both sideways and longitudinally. Loss of balance longitudinally refers to the young horse's frequent changes in speed both by changing the rhythm of his stride and by changing its length. Often young horses will move in the manner of runaways, changing rapidly to joltingly slow, even hesitant strides. To these activities, horses often add discomfort caused by drifting sideways. A horse can, and will, drift in his totality or in bits and pieces, such as when leaning toward a shoulder or pushing his haunches to one side.

With such horses the patterns for helping, indeed, should be a lack of patterns. Instead, the rider must skillfully accompany the horse's drifting as well as sudden shifts in speed and stride. The rider must build the horse's confidence by not getting in his way, which includes not demanding exacting, man-made patterns. How could a young horse possibly understand, let alone physically deal with, even the simplest suggestion of going straight along a wall, bending through a corner and then straightening again for the next wall, and do all this in perfect balance, with metronomic rhythmic regularity and great impulsion. Such hopes must wait and are, indeed, the goals and purposes of careful training.

Once a horse has understood that his rider will not allow a separation of their respective centers of gravity, that his rider has remained part and parcel of him, then the rider can gradually give the horse pattern-controlling directions as an "insider." The horse must always have the confidence that his rider understands and shares his, the horse's, point of view. He should also feel that his rider can and will remain in harmony with him and participate in the "dancing partnership" of two highly unlikely structures.

The basic exercises and simple patterns appropriate for young, untrained horses should be reviewed for longer or shorter periods even on the most advanced horses. The proportion of simple foundation work will change depending on sophistication of skills and strength. As a horse advances, one merely has to review the fundamentals and basics but not fill the entire training period with them.

A dressage arena may be the most ideal training facility for most horses during most of their athletic life. However, it is not sufficient to be the only training area. All horses should move outdoors in natural surroundings throughout their lives for reasons of work (acquisition of special skills and strength) and recreation, relaxation and mental resting. Ideally, dressage arenas should have the complement of a "great canter track" or at least a modified facsimile of one. As much as available space permits, one must develop a large and wide track for training around the outer perimeter of one's available property.

Daily work should, on any level, be started on this large track where the horse can move forward with minimum hindrance and certainly without inhibiting the grandeur of his natural gaits. The patterns at the beginning of training and later at the beginning of each daily session should really be a lack of patterns. Horses should be warmed up and even limbered by being "ridden through their toplines" on these large tracks prior to submitting them to patterns, all of which would demand more collection from them.

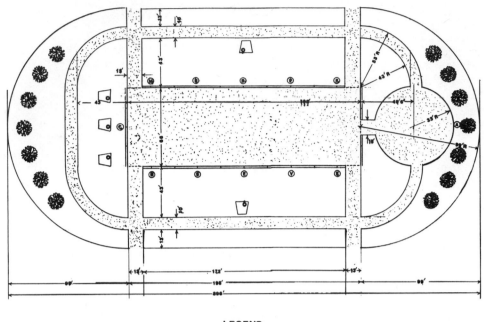

LEGEND

RIDING AREAS		LARGE SHRUBS OR TREES
PERIMETER FENCE OF ARENA		LOW GROUND COVER
REMOVABLE FENCE		
PLACEMENT OF JUDGES		0 5 10 25 50
JUDGES' ENCLOSURES		FEET

This training and competition area is designed to make for a good environment in a restricted space. Even in the smallest riding areas care should be taken to have a so-called large canter ring follow as close to the perimeter of the available space as possible. Here the standard manege is placed in the middle of the complex. Notice the large oval track that allows horses to start long and low and to limber up by moving forward as unrestrictedly as possible and in as long a frame as possible. The horse, first of all, must be an athlete. To build an athlete one needs space for continuously flowing movement. Respiration, strength and forward will all come from seeing as few corners as possible.

Ideally, horses should be ridden out of the arena several times a week. The confinement of the manege can be both boring and stressful to the horse. He needs variety, roomy work areas and to be out in nature. Often this is not possible. Also, to ride outdoors and freely, riders must go in company and must be very accomplished in their riding skills. These requirements preclude the majority of passionate riders from going out into the countryside. Yet on a nice large path, such as shown in this illustration, everything that could be done in cross-country riding can still be attained here.   Design copyright by Charles de Kunffy. Graphics: Richard F. Williams.

CHANGING REIN

Changing rein, of course, refers to changing direction. This particular *terminus technicus* (technical terminology), however, should hold our attention for a moment. The expression comes from the age-old custom of riding the horse on the inside rein! The expression "to trot on the left rein," for instance, referred to a horse moving with his left side to the inside while his rider was primarily guiding and controlling him with his left, therefore, inside rein. A command to canter on the left rein meant a canter on the left lead.

The contemporary preoccupation of demanding riders to ride their horses from "inside leg to outside rein" is in direct opposition to the suggestions of these age-old terminologies. Elsewhere I address this issue further. I agree that the horse developed enough to work in collection (particularly flexibility and articulation at his hocks) can and will contact the rider's outside rein (thereby releasing, if not slacking, the feeling in the inside one) when correctly engaged by the rider's inside driving (and timing) leg. The key to understanding this concept is being aware (1) that the horse has to be developed (advanced) to collected work; (2) that it is the horse who *contacts*, and not the rider who pulls, the outside rein; and (3) it happens only when the driving influences of the inside leg engage the horse's inside leg forward, rather than displacing it sideways across producing an unwanted leg-yield.

Changing rein (direction) is very important for the horse if he is to develop into an ambidextrous athlete. For younger horses, frequent changes of direction allow the hind legs to rest alternatively; or conversely, to work more with alternating hind legs. Horses work more (and develop more) the hind leg that is on the inside because that leg often bears more weight and always has the responsibility of being the "shock absorber." Later, when the horse has developed athletically and is stronger, changes of rein continue to play an important role. They help even up the length and height of the strides made by each hind leg and therefore contribute to efforts in straightening and balancing the horse.

Riders benefit from frequent changes of riding direction

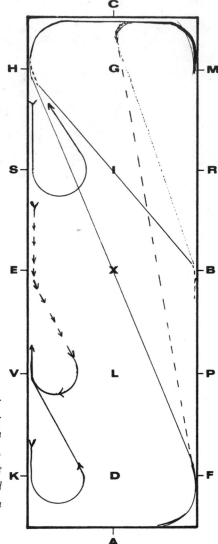

When considering patterns for change of rein it is essential that they all start with a horse bent in one direction, then straighten absolutely (like a ruler) the horse's spine and finally bend in the new direction of going.

also. In this book you will notice that each pattern we ride will be evaluated on its usefulness for both horse and rider. Riders learn exactitude in controlling their horses. Their skills in bending the horse one way and then the opposite way with intermediary straight strides develop, and these skills are at the heart of the controls necessary for developing an ambidextrous horse that moves straight and with an even loading (use) of his hind legs.

The simplest and also the most commonly used changes of direction occur on diagonal lines. (See illustration on page 48.) A horse changing rein from H to F on the diagonal will benefit from the following specific work. In the corner before H the rider has a chance to half-halt, rebalance his horse and put the "springs" under him before the longest straight path of the arena begins. There the horse should be geometrically (versus functionally) as straight as possible in his spine and move rhythmically without losing balance. The corner after F also must be prepared for with half-halt and the proper positional changes of the rider to facilitate the new bending to the right. Because the diagonal is the longest straight line in the manege, it is the one most often chosen to train (encourage) the lengthening of the strides in the walk and in the trot. For lengthening canter strides, the diagonal is appropriate only for advanced horses that can deliver flying changes of leads. Riders can utilize the horse's natural tendency to stride freer and longer on long paths to develop lengthening and eventually extended gaits. However, diagonals should be ridden with a relative (to the horse's development) degree of collection in order to discourage anticipation and to take advantage of the natural forward tendencies that are so necessary for successful collection.

Riders should be aware that horses, being born more or less crooked, will choose to "drift" on the diagonal toward one or the other of their shoulders. Horses working at the basic levels will "drift upstream" or "drift downstream" before reaching "the opposite shore" of the manege.

You can discourage drifting by applying the appropriate straightening aids, and also by changing rein halfway through the arena, for example, from H to B (see page 48). Even more control will be necessary when you change from the center line to either the end of the long wall, such as a change from C to F, or from the center line to the middle of the long wall, as from C to B.

Diagonal changes can be sophisticated to small patterns that start with half a volte and return with a few straight strides back to the original wall. This movement can most easily be controlled by starting it in a corner, such as at K, demivolte (half-circle with 6m diameter) and returning to the rail at V (see page 48).

More sophisticated placement would start the demivolte at S and return to H (see page 48).

Riding "counter patterns" can be a highly educational experience for the rider, who is forced by these patterns to ride more exacting patterns. Most patterning is from the walls of the manege inward. However, when we leave the wall to execute a pattern outward, we can call it a "counter pattern." We can reverse some of our suggested changes of reins and create a counter pattern: for example, departing the wall at E (traveling on the left rein) to the quarter line (5m from wall) of the arena and then ride the half-volte to the right, arriving at V facing in the other direction (see page 48). In this as in most other counter patterns, horse and rider cannot "cheat" on the demands by enlarging the half-volte because the wall "forces" its correctly small size. However, if the horse is not yet ready to work on precision, we should instead continue to school him with "true patterns" inward from the wall. This will allow us to make patterns appropriately larger in order to save the horse's perfection (clarity) of gaits and exactitude of rhythm, both of which are far more important than the intricacy of a small, difficult pattern. After all, patterns are for schooling better gaits and for evaluating the results of that schooling. Patterns should never be used to drill exactitude at the expense of gaits with suspension, elasticity and rhythm.

The changes of reins discussed so far have one thing in common: they start with bending, use a straight line for directional change and result in positioning or bending in the new (opposite) direction. The straight part of the pattern is always diagonal (see page 48).

Somewhat more sophisticated controls are needed to change direction on the center line, such as from C to A, or on the half arena line, such as from E to B. (See illustration on page 51.) Obviously these two basic patterns can be varied slightly to forestall anticipation or to sophisticate the challenge by riding them on the available parallel lines. For instance, instead of changing rein by coming down on the center line, you can turn with a demivolte onto the quarter line and ride the length of the arena on it, turning in the opposite direction at the end of the line as you reach the opposite short wall. Similarly, instead of

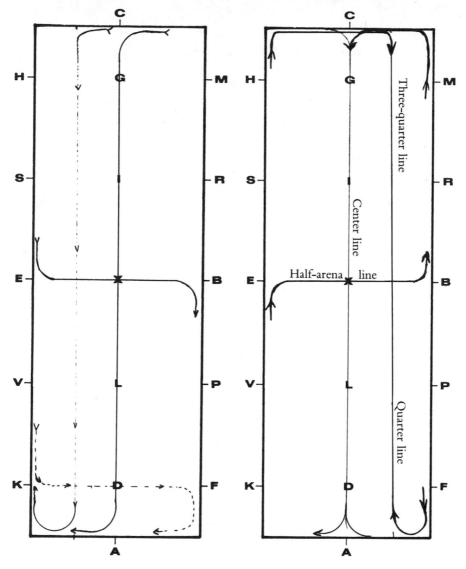

Both the center line and the half-arena line divide the arena into two equal parts. They are very commonly used in patterns, for example, to proceed on them straight or to go to them either on one track or sideways on two tracks. The quarter lines (there are two of them, between either long wall and the center line) can be called the quarter or the three quarter, depending on the point from which they are approached. Quarter lines are very useful to know about, especially when you need to ride counter patterns. For instance, from the three-quarter line you could turn toward the wall closest to it. By riding such a small, outward turn, the size of the pattern cannot be enlarged, thereby making the movement easier. For the wall itself will insure that the pattern remains the desired size.

changing rein on the half arena line, you can cross from one long wall to the other, from S to R or from V to P, or on an advanced horse, from K to F.

For purposes of gymnastic development and correction, riders should carefully select, when changing rein, which one of the bendings on either end of the straight pattern will be the tighter or more difficult one to ride. If you trot on the left rein along the long wall and change rein by turning left at K and turning right at F, the second bending to the right will be far more difficult to prepare for and execute than the bending at K, where ample preparations (half-halts and positioning) were possible.

It is possible to change reins on continuous bent lines as well. This category of changing is generally more demanding of the horse gymnastically and far more skill-demanding of the rider than were the preceding changes, all of which included straight lines.

Riding serpentines with an even number of loops will facilitate a change of rein. The simplest of these would be a serpentine of two loops, or an S-curve. In a small arena measuring 20m by 40m, such an S-curve can easily be formed by riding from C to X a half-circle of 20m diameter, followed by another half-circle of same size from X to A. When changing direction and with it the horse's bending, ideally you should ride at least one stride absolutely straight before re-bending the horse in the new direction.

All serpentines become more sophisticated as we diminish the radius of the half-circles that constitute their loops. Picture the regular-size competition dressage arena: in it, we can ride a serpentine of four loops from C to A with all straightening movements made when the horse crosses the center line by tracking over it at exactly 90 degrees (i.e., perpendicular to the center line). This serpentine is best ridden wall to wall. As the horse advances and needs more sophisticated strengthening and suppling (by more intense lateral bending) exercises, these serpentine loops should be ridden smaller. For instance, a serpentine consisting of six loops ridden from wall to wall will bend the horse on a pattern that includes all the loops greater than just half a circle, and the straight strides preceding the changes of direction

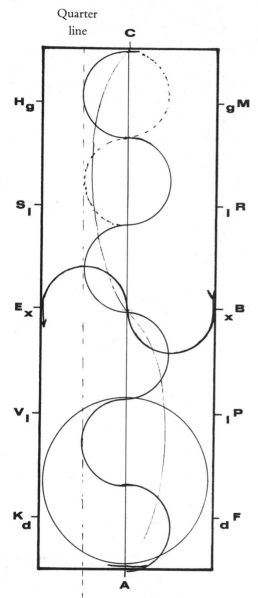

Quarter line

Serpentines are very difficult to execute—those illustrated here or any other. Nothing proves suppleness, flexibility and—strangely—straightness of the horse better than the ability to flow through the lateral bending changes from side to side, without crossing legs, throwing a shoulder outward (bulging) or cutting with a shoulder inward (leaning). If a horse can alternately bend in motion without losing balance, rhythm, cadence and impulsion, you have proof of excellent work.

will cross the center line slightly diagonally. That is, the center line will not be intercepted at exactly 90 degrees. However, the six-loop serpentine can be performed between the two quarter lines with 90-degree crossing of the center line. (See illustration above.) To further intensify the bending of the torso and flexing of the haunches, you can ride four- or six-loop serpentines between the long wall and the center line or between the two quarter lines. The variety of pattern vocabulary is endless. Depending on the rider's imagination, basic pattern ideas can be varied infinitely and also changed in their value by making them smaller (more difficult, of course) or larger.

Working on a 20m diameter circle (the width of the dressage arena) is fundamental to the development of any horse. This will be discussed in detail later. For now, let me remind you that the greatest use of the S-curve for changing rein is, indeed, when riding through the center of a 20m circle. The change of rein through the circle is one of the most important suppling exercises (see page 53). When it causes difficulties (as it always will initially) by disturbing the rhythm and suspension of the gait in one direction, the rider should use 10m circles as a corrective exercise. For example, you are riding on the right-hand side on a 20m circle when you decide to change through the circle with an S-curve. The first bending to the right (half-circle of 10m diameter) will be fairly easy since most horses tend to "hollow" more easily to the right. I purposely do not label this "bending better" to the right, for bending must be continuous and the hind legs must load evenly forward. Most horses hollow to the right by bending more with their neck than with the torso, pushing the left shoulder outward (off the circle) and crossing the right hind leg as if in a "mini" leg-yield. These are all evasions of bending rather than a successful demonstration of it. Still the half-circle is smoother sailing to the right and more easily corrigible by the rider's aids. However, at the center of the circle we must bend the horse left onto the second half-circle, which completes the changing of his direction. Most horses are stiffer to the left and therefore must develop (not switch on) his bending in that direction. Here is the value of discontinuing a pattern temporarily, for reasons of correction, until one can return to the original design and succeed with it in substance and not just superficial form.

The corrective measures for improving bending for the change of rein through the S-curve is to ride continuously on a 10m circle until we succeed in bending our horse properly onto it. Then carefully prepare the change of direction, and even encourage a few steps of counter flexion before changing direction. If in the new direction the horse falls on his inside shoulder, or speeds up, or stiffens, we remain on the circle in that direction until we improve his bending. Then, again attempt the change of direction through an S-curve.

Serpentines are patterns with more virtues than just changing the horse's lateral bending and his direction of going. You can modify serpentines to increase their gymnastic value. The most useful elaborations on serpentines include the riding of the apexes of half-circles at a shoulder-in, or while riding toward the center line do a leg-yield off the new inside leg. This will help to establish bending toward the new direction.

Seven

Longitudinal Exercises

Longitudinal exercises are based on the successful longitudinal flexion of the horse and are designed to promote suppleness. While improving ligamental elasticity by stretching and contracting, they also supple the musculature by encouraging its expansion (on one side) and contraction (usually on the opposite side). Since the horse's skeleton itself is moved by muscles, it is very important to understand how the musculature works and how it is built for both strength and elasticity.

In addition to their suppling properties, longitudinal exercises also contribute to the horse's balance. Balancing a horse is much more complex than we think because the horse's balance must and will shift with almost every step. The rider's perpetual goal is to shift the horse's center of gravity toward his haunches as much as possible. There are few synonyms for "good riding," but one may well be the ability to "collect" a horse. Collection is always proportionate to the degree of the horse's shifting his center of gravity toward his haunches. All riding aspires to liberate the forehand and to anchor the horse's balance toward his haunches. This enables the horse to work more efficiently with his haunches—the source of all propellant energy.

Arthur Kottas-Heldenberg, Chief Rider of the Spanish Riding School in Vienna, Austria, is riding his horse in great collection. It is obvious that the horse "hangs down from the rider's seat" and is free to engage his haunches with utmost articulation in the joints. Notice that even the horse's left hip appears "sunken." All joints bend. The liberated forehand lifts elegantly to twice the height of the hind hoof's trajectory.

The rider is not only one of the best in the world but certainly one of the few extremely elegant ones. Elegance is born of a combination of emotions made visible and of the absolute perfection of correct (not corrupted!) riding skills. His hands are visibly those of a giver and not those of a miser. Horse and rider appear to be in a state of meditation, both of them having lost themselves to be found in the other. The horse finds himself in the rider's will and the rider in the horse's power.

This is collection, a shifting of the center of gravity toward the haunches to permit carriage rather than locomotion. Slow and graceful but optimally active through the articulation of joints.   Photo: Andreas Jarc.

As the weight-bearing abilities of the haunches increase, the horse can work with greater efficiency, which will result in "carrying his rider" forward by lifting, rather than running forward with the rider by pushing. Nature did not intend the horse to bear additional weight on his back, so the rider must create the conditions by which the horse can carry a rider without damaging himself.

Exercises that improve longitudinal balance, and as a consequence flexion, include all the transitions. There are two categories of transitions: changing from one gait to another and lengthening or elevating the stride.

In the first category, riders ask their horses to move from one gait to another. When making such transitions riders are aware of two subcategories: "shifting up" to a potentially faster tempo (gait) and "shifting down" to a potentially slower gait. I emphasize the concept of "potentially" faster or slower gaits. Gaits are only "potentially" faster or slower because a well-gymnasticized horse will be able to canter slower than he can walk (school canter vs. extended walk), for instance. In nature, the slowest gait, when unschooled, is the walk, the middle speed potential is for the trot and the greatest potential speed can be reached at the canter.

We must not dwell on the meaning of the gallop, which is fast and is actually a different gait from the canter. It has a different footfall sequence from that of the canter. Since the gallop is not one of the usual schooling movements and certainly not performed in a manege, I will not be discussing it.

The most important aspect of transitions from one gait to another is the clarity and purity of each transition. This means that the last stride of the abandoned gait must be as clear, wholesome and perfect as any that preceded it. And the first stride of the new gait must be as clear, balanced, steady and correct as any that may follow it. There must be a clear demarcation from one gait to the other without compromised, deteriorated and muddled intermediary strides between them. In essence, good transitions do not "develop" another gait but create it at once without transitional compromises.

During each transition the horse should be asked to shift

his center of gravity toward the haunches. When you "shift" from a 9 mph canter to a 3 mph walk, the horse will have to shift his center of gravity toward the haunches. After all, any kind of speed reduction must produce such a gravitational change. Therefore, "downward shifting" transitions are "natural" collecting exercises. But we must also school our horse to shift his center of gravity toward the haunches even prior to changing to gaits of greater tempo. The transitions "upward," therefore, must be preceded by a half-halt, which collects the horse before he is permitted to stride in the new gait. Both upward and downward transitions greatly strengthen the haunches and, as any gymnastic endeavor when well done, strengthen the whole system. We cannot think about horses, or for that matter riders, as bits and pieces. They work and develop as whole organisms. Each "part" affects all the others!

In the second category, more sophisticated transitions involve those that either lengthen or elevate (that is, to shorten by collecting) the strides of horses with the same gait. When we school the basic gaits, we are aware of each one as "ordinary" in the way the horse naturally offers it to the rider. Knowing fully what the ordinary gaits represent, we must train away from them and improve upon them. We ride horses in working, medium, extended and collected gaits but never in the ordinary ways they volunteer. All of the gaits that represent improvement by the rider over the ordinary gaits offered by the horse are improvements by virtue of their "magnifying" the horse's ordinary offer. Not only the extensions but more importantly the collections should also represent a "magnification" of the gaits (walk, trot or canter) by virtue of elevation of the strides and articulation of the horse's joints.

In brief, all longitudinal exercises aim to control the horse's ability to shift his center of gravity toward his haunches and to foster his ability to magnify his gaits either in the direction of maximum length or in the direction of maximum height of stride. All transitions increase the horse's strength in his muscles (through elasticity) and in his joints (through suppleness). All transitions aim to improve (not break down) the clarity and definition of the gaits.

THE ATHLETIC DEVELOPMENT OF THE DRESSAGE HORSE

Susan Derr Drake is riding the Hanoverian Parmenio at the trot. Notice the vast differences in the trot in each of these photographs. Opposite above, the horse is moving in a medium trot. The strides are extended, relative to the working trot, yet show great power to lift as a sense of collection toward the haunches is retained. The medium gaits are always a fascinating mixture of an extension with great suspension and therefore height of motion. This trot is powerful in both dimensions: horizontally, for being extended, and vertically, by being cadenced into high suspension. This medium trot is the "bread-and-butter" movement for any development toward international dressage competition. From it, by allowing the utmost stretching of limbs and body, can issue the extended trot. Or by collecting it suddenly and cadencing it, it will become the majestic passage, the most thrilling of collected trots for its sustained suspension that allows for floating.

Opposite below, the horse is at an extended trot. Now allowed to stretch fully forward both his forearm and neck, his hind legs can reach forward to the greatest length in overstriding the hoofprints left behind by the forehand. Notice the powerful thrust of the haunches, the "lumbar tucking," the tilting of the pelvis forward, making the length of strides as vast as structurally possible, without exchanging carriage for a dash on the forehand. While fully extending his limbs to reach, the horse remains on his haunches.

Above, an elegantly floating passage. Brilliantly unusual is the rider's ability to produce collection and cadence without "compacting" the horse's neck. In fact, the horse is elevated at his poll without any attempt to confine his neck and inhibit his haunches by the hands. This, then, is a wonderful example that collection never "gathers up" from the hands.

These three pictures of Susan Derr Drake and Parmenio offer a brief visual summary of one of the most important training principles: that the purity of gaits must be maintained and that its success is proven by the horse being able to move at a medium trot and enabling the rider to choose whether to maximize length into extension or maximize verticality into passage. Notice that in all three modes of behavior you can find the consistency in active haunches, great suspension, lightness in the forehand and balance, insuring carriage rather than a "fall" to the forehand.

Photo: Paul Drake.

Specific exercises for longitudinal development fall into two categories. The common feature of each is that the exercises work the horse in "accordion" fashion, that is, producing elasticity through expansion and contraction. The two areas we are able to affect are the musculature and the skeleton. As the first exercise is to elasticize—expand and contract—the musculature, we must keep the horse's strides absolutely even—even in rhythm and even in length of reach and height of lift. What we alter is the outline of the horse's body. We stretch the horse as long as possible by inducing the stretching of his neck and by persuading him to stretch his head forward and down. His whole body will then be carried as long as physically possible by a totally stretched spinal column as the musculature expands. The topline is rounded by the elevation of the back, the stretched spine allows a swinging "articulation" in the motion of the horse's back. Then, we can gradually gather the horse's frame so he contracts his muscles without stiffening himself. This should result in a spine that is still stretched, but one that is now more intensely curved to allow for a highly arched, gracefully carried neck, a greater tucking of the pelvis under, and a rounding of the lower back. This helps push the hind legs further under and more forward relative to the location of the hip. In short, we lengthen and stretch the horse's topline, without losing its—however mild—flexion. Then we, alternately, contract the horse's body into a much shorter, more compact position in which the head in particular is raised higher by virtue of the pelvis being tucked forward and under. All through these changes in silhouette the horse's footfalls must remain identical both in rhythm and reach.

The second "accordion" exercise to complement the one just described is based on lengthening and shortening the horse's strides (the underpinnings, or the "base" of the horse) without altering his outline. This accordion effect has great strengthening value for the skeletal development of the horse, meaning the elasticity, suppleness, and therefore strength of his joints. The activity, articulation, flexibility and bending of the joints increases as the horse is asked to stride a great deal longer or a great deal taller (and, coincidentally, shorter), while maintaining an unchanged silhouette!

The important concept to understand about "accordion"

Above, the period of suspension in the medium trot superbly illustrated by Susan Derr Drake riding Parmenio. Absolutely synchronized diagonal pairs of legs are moving faultlessly in the cleanest of two beats needed for proper trotting. This period of suspension is essential for the definition of the trot! When the suspension is as tall and the strides are as long as shown here, we see the medium trot at its best. But we also see the meaning of carriage. The horse lifts his rider off the ground, which he uses merely as a trampoline.

Below, the period of suspension at the extended trot. The horse stretches longer with both his legs and his body. A lower silhouette for the neck, as it too must slightly extend, is ideal as here presented by the same horse and rider. Compare the medium and extended trots while both are suspended at the moment of their brilliance. The medium is taller, the extended is longer!

Extending the trot in good balance is difficult enough. Doing so on a circle is one of the most daring exercises. Yet we must do it to develop the gymnastically indispensable balance and engagement of the horse. Here Elizabeth Ball is riding Bolshoj in that wonderful kind of circle which becomes a "point in motion returning to its origin" simply because the horse is absolutely correctly bent evenly from poll to tail. Photo: Richard F. Williams.

exercises is that a horse in motion develops only when he is dynamic (ever changing) in either length of body or in length of stride or, ultimately, in a combination of both! A horse held together or ridden in a perpetually static outline or mechanical footfall will never develop gymnastically. Instead the mechanical puppet will look emaciated, stiff and "nailed to the bit" with an artificial outline that looks impossible to alter. Looseness denied, suppleness and elasticity unknown, the horse takes the form of trained automaton but does not represent the substance of a happily developed, proud athlete. Only a horse exhibiting elasticity of underpinnings and topline can continue to grow athletically toward perfection.

Let me suggest a few "accordion" patterns that may stimulate more ideas and more creative work. For instance, at the trot lengthen the strides on the long walls and shorten them on the short walls. Make sure that "successful" half-halts precede the corners, for both the sake of bending and for changing the length of the stride. As an elaboration on this simple pattern, you can make a 20m circle (on more advanced horses, 10m), while collecting in front of both A and C. Much more difficult would be the exercise of lengthening stride for only as long as the distance between two consecutive letters and then shorten the stride between the next two consecutive letters. For example, lengthen from F to P and shorten from P to B, and so on.

A similar level of difficulty involves the lengthening and shortening of strides alternately on a 20m circle. This longitudinal "activating" exercise is highly sophisticated because the horse must remain bent and laterally balanced while performing it. It's best is to attempt exactitude while not sacrificing purity of gait or balance. Make an exact plan about which half-circle will be longer and which half will be shorter in stride. This will build good riding habits and can be used, as exactitude always can, to determine a rider's effectiveness and a horse's obedience.

Let us remember that we have a "second accordion" to play: We can keep the strides even in length but alternately lengthen and shorten our horse's frame! We can use plans similar or identical to those above to determine where we wish to facilitate the changes.

Eight

The Importance of the Circle

There can be no development of the horse's athletic abilities without gymnasticizing in the manege because a well-defined, lettered manege allows, encourages and finally succeeds in training with exactitude to constantly monitor the effectiveness of this training by checking on the horse's level of obedience. We cannot monitor the horse's understanding of our communications, we cannot evaluate his physical progress in balance and suppleness or engagement and collection without moving on precisely defined patterns.

Cross-country riding can build strength, stamina, heart and lungs. It can also strengthen muscles and joints and "leg up the horse" and give him improved respiration. Skills, awareness, stamina and more can be built by cross country jumping, especially. Cavalletti work improves observation, obedience, rhythm, elevation of strides, suspension, stretching, elasticity and more. Yet without the manege, and without exacting patterns, the horse cannot be precisely evaluated.

Of all the patterns available, none is more important than the circle when riding on a single track. In fact we either ride straight or on a partial arc or full circle. When we ride on a straight pattern we are not always riding a geometrically straight horse whose spine is kept straight and whose hind legs load exactly evenly both forward and upward (length of stride and elevation or articulation). Instead, often we ride a bent horse along a straight line. All two-track movements, such as the shoulder-in and -out or the haunches-in or -out or the half-passes, are most often ridden along straight paths yet on two separate tracks, one for the haunches, the other for the forehand. In essence, a very small percentage of all manege riding is ever done on a straight path with a straight horse, and even then it is interrupted frequently by the bent corners. Conversely, the majority of all riding is done on curving paths (circles or parts of them) and with a laterally bent horse. Classical equitation demands, indeed insists, on riding horses bent exactly and continuously parallel over the path on which they move. The counter patterns are the well-designed, much-needed, schooling exceptions to this traditional rule for the bending of the horse parallel to his path of progression. The reason for the insistence on bending is the horse's need for "shock absorbers" as he impacts on the ground with the additional weight of rider and saddlery.

One sees very few circles correctly guided by the rider and therefore one sees very few horses performing a correct circle. When a circle is correctly performed by a horse, it is a consequence of a precise, even, continuous spinal bending maintained while in motion. Locomotion plus correct body curvature simply creates the circle. Consequently, riders should not visually search for the pattern for the circle on the sand, as many do with scanning head and the resultant displacement of their center of gravity and all aids. Instead, riders should "feel the circle" when a well-bent horse in good balance and impulsion simply returns to the point of his origin without any "steering efforts" at all! The surprise comes when it happens well; indeed, circles can be ridden well with all reins in one hand and no steering but, instead, aiding for bending, balance, rhythm and impulsion.

THE BENEFITS OF THE CIRCLE

Let us examine the special benefits rather than the general use-fulness of the circle.

Riding a circle is the most effective solution to shying. The worst a rider can do is to slow down or even halt to "show and tell" the horse about the object of his concern. A good rider should move into the horse's mind, his "psychology," and know that shying is most often a pretense, used to get out of work! Shying, not coincidentally, occurs when the demand increases, such as during extensions, piaffe or the like. Seldom will a horse shy when walking on a diagonal on a loose rein! After all, horses are not afraid of things, and they do sleep alone in the dark. If a rider permits slowing and looking at the object of the pretended fear, the horse gets what he wants: "a cigarette break" from work. He is rewarded by underwork or even a restful halt. We underestimate the importance that halting has for horses, because for them it is more than just standing. Horses can and do sleep while standing. To allow them to stand and look is a great reward and a sign that you to allow a "nap" posture to replace work.

This has much to do with the circle. Riding a circle corrects and eventually eliminates shying. On a circle the horse will move halfway around away from the object of his concern; only on the other half will he need to be forced toward the object of his often pretended fear. On the way toward the point of shying the rider must speed up his horse. The lesson is that we forget, temporarily, about rhythm, lack of tension, elasticity and all that because we are addressing the "mind of the pupil." We work harder! Shying means double work. We speed, even run, toward the fear–object. This is one of the few times when "run along" is agreeable as a goal. On the half-circle departing from the object of fear, however, we relax, we adjust the horse's balance, we gently praise him by stroking his neck, and we become agreeable companions. As the circle is repeated, we should mellow our insistence in pushing toward the fear-object and allow the horse to "pretend" also that he actually never noticed anything in particular there anyway. By repeatedly riding a circle in front of a fear-object, we inevitably produce the desired result: The horse will ignore it, offering submission to our aids, giving full attention to our commands and surrendering the haunches to work as usual.

In addition to the simple task of repeatedly bringing the horse alternately toward and away from the object of fear, the circle allows us to increase the horse's submission through his inside hind leg. Propose a leg-yield first, later even a shoulder-in on the half-circle approaching the feared object, while allowing a straight and relaxed "flight away from it" on the other arc. For the horse "lives in his haunches" and not in his head; he is where his haunches are, not where his muzzle is. Therefore, pulling a horse toward the fear-object is the worst thing a rider can do. Conversely, riding his haunches, with a leg-yield or shoulder-in toward the object, is the most beneficial. If the haunches approach a point, the horse "gets there." If only the head points to a certain place, the horse is not necessarily "there." His haunches can pivot inward and drift away from our control, and thus drifts the horse's mind, his attention and his respect for the rider!

Circles are great strengthening patterns. The horse's hind legs work more, especially at the hocks, when balancing on a circle. The gymnastic value of circles will greatly improve if their size is changed by spiraling inward and outward. The resulting suppling of the joints is paralleled by an increase in muscular elasticity as well. On a circle a horse must contract his muscles on the inside of his body (closest to the center of the circle) and stretch (expand) his muscles on the outside. He will also need to push his back muscles up on the outside slightly more than on the inner side.

Spiraling is best done by smoothly and gradually diminishing the size of a circle. Think of the needle of a phonograph moving gradually inward on a record toward its center. Usually, we should start with a 20m circle and reduce it to one of 10m in diameter. Then gradually we should spiral out (unfortunately, no phonograph analogy is possible) and enlarge our circle to the original 20m. The rider benefits by being careful to do this difficult task with legs and seat only and should not steer or pull the horse inward or outward with the hands.

As always in good horsemanship, the first few times we ride a pattern we consider its usefulness mostly diagnostic. We learn which way the horse might drift, stiffen or make mistakes in rhythm and balancing. Then we address these issues as we repeat the pattern. This is "patterning history." First diagnose, then correct each of the shortcomings you may have noted. With practice, the rider will master his control of the patterns and the horse will gain the strength, skills and understanding of how to do them outstandingly. Then athletic growth commences.

Spiraling in and out can be done, experimentally, with all reins in one hand. Even when that is unnecessary, the rider must be committed to performing spirals inward off the pressure from the outside leg and outward as a result of engagement from his inside leg. Thus it will become natural for us to elaborate on the spirals to make them more therapeutically corrective of a problem or more athletically developmental when no corrections are in fact needed.

One can elaborate by diminishing the circle with a haunches-in, i.e., the haunches slightly leading and enlarging the circle by riding outward on a drift, which can either be a leg-yield or a shoulder-in. Depending on the horse's development, one can make spiraling a very sophisticated attempt at collection (rebalancing toward the haunches) or a sophisticated way of increasing lateral bending. The possibilities are endless as one combines the inward movement either on a single track or on two tracks, which may include, in addition to haunches-in, a counter flexion which gives us a shoulder-out. Increasing the circle can also be endlessly varied, as it is combined into single- or two-track ways of proceeding outward.

Since the spiral enables the horse to learn more leg crossing and more body bending, its gymnastic value is staggering when the benefits are tallied up. Spirals help with balance, elasticity and suppleness as few other exercises can. Spiraling must be regarded with caution because of its tendency to diminish impulsion, disturb rhythmic regularity and sharply drop the amount of suspension. But then again, an alert and knowledgeable rider will know that all collection and bending exercises should be immediately followed by straight patterns and extensions to reacquaint the horse with the well-known lessons about "maximizing" the gaits and that progression is always forward, even and straight!

PATTERNING FOR LATERAL BENDING

To straighten a horse and ride it forward is the ultimate goal of dressage. The means to attaining this end, however, include the lateral bending of the horse. Before suggesting some useful gymnastic patterns for lateral work, let me remind you of the most important general principles.

There are two kinds of lateral work: that which is performed on a single track and that which is performed on two tracks.

Lateral Exercises Performed on a Single Track

The arc, or any portion of a circle, is usually the standardized 20m, 15m, 10m, 8m or 6m diameter circle. Each corner of the arena should be ridden as an arc, simply because it is one and therein lies the gymnastic value in riding corners. As always, the larger the arc ridden, the easier it is, but its strengthening, suppling and balancing value is lessened accordingly.

The circle should be ridden with as much exactitude as possible on one of the standardized sizes. Habits, both human and equine, are formed and perpetuated by each pattern performed. Rider precision and the resulting horse obedience are invaluable assets in the gymnastic development of the horse. Depending upon the size of the circle, the horse should be bent laterally accordingly. Remember that the circle is not merely an imagined geometric shape upon the ground. It should rather be a by-product of a properly (even and continuously) bent horse that is traveling in good balance, impeccable rhythm and proper length as well as suspension of strides. As a result of a well-traveling horse at a certain degree of bending, we should coincidentally perform a perfect circle, which will not be an imagined geometric shape, but a performed actuality.

Serpentines are difficult gymnastically because the not-too-flexible horse is asked to change lateral bending rapidly, ideally, within one straight step. With the changing of lateral bending, all else changes for the horse. His center of gravity relocates (to the side of the spine closest to the hollow) and consequently the use of his limbs is immediately modified. Depending on the gait (walk, trot or canter) and the length of stride expected, a great deal of stress can be put on the inside hind leg, particularly on the hock. Since everything changes radically when the bending of the horse changes, a serpentine is obviously an exercise of great complexity that demands skill and dexterity from both rider and horse. Even a generously sized serpentine is demanding, therefore we must know how one with many small loops and frequent directional (and bending) changes can become a sophisticated training challenge. Teaching serpentines to horses and riders should include corrective measures. One, for example, is to precede the change of direction by a few steps of counter bending. That is, bend the horse against the curvature of the arc on which you move, and ride him "bent wrong" before changing direction. In this exercise the horse is bent laterally onto the arc of the new direction before he reaches the center line. In essence, you are prematurely bending the horse onto the arc on which he will, within a few steps, arrive. First shape the horse and then let the pattern unfold.

The other corrective measure is refusing to change direction on a serpentine until we know the horse is balanced and straightened for at least one step and is therefore ready to change both his bending and his direction. If that feeling in the rider is not confirmed, the horse should be kept moving on a circle that has the same diameter as the loops of the serpentine. When the horse is bent in fine balance and rhythm onto the circle, then we must negotiate his reshaping to accommodate the opposite bending that will put him on the next loop of the serpentine.

The figure-8 is also a complex pattern because the horse must change his bending, such as he did during a serpentine, within one straight stride, at the meeting point of the two circles. However, in this exercise the complications involve the horse's inborn crookedness, or one-sidedness. He will offer one circle with too much neck bending, the outside shoulder pushed outward (traveling like a tricycle with one wheel in front at the center and two wheels straddling it behind). Or if his shoulder is successfully controlled, he might opt for the evasion of a slight haunches-in. Some horses manage to combine both evasions. This is aggravated by problems of the horse refusing to contact the bit on the hollow (inside) side and pulling too much on the outer side. To the other side (usually left) the horse will be reluctant to offer any bending and therefore will move nearly straight or even counter-bent. This often fools his rider into pulling more on the inside rein to keep up the illusion of bending in lieu of the real thing. Here the horse will tend to swing the haunches outward, off the curvature of the arc, and assist himself in this wrongdoing by also crossing with the inside hind leg in the style of a leg-yielding to facilitate the spinning out at the haunches. The crossing inside leg (usually left on a left circle) will, of course, refuse forward support (loading) in the direction of the left forehand.

While schooling a horse in the figure-8 we have a chance to repeat two circles, in opposite directions and with opposite lateral bending expected from the horse. The fast and frequent repetition of these circles affords the rider good observational (diagnostic) opportunities and repeated chances to correct his horse's various evasive maneuvers to avoid proper bending.

Perhaps now is the appropriate time to note that horses are not conspiratorial animals. In fact, they lack all analytical faculties and cannot conceptualize the wait-a-minute strategy of conspiratorial humans. It is a grave mistake to attribute anthropomorphic characteristics to the horse and yet never use time and imagination to learn how he really might feel.

Horses evade by changing speed (usually to run but sometimes to plant their feet!) and by going crooked. The latter means, of course, any evasion of the rider's attempts to place the horse's spine in a parallel position over the pattern on which he moves. Also, when a horse is crooked he will, because of anatomic limitations, be incapable of loading evenly with his hind legs and therefore incapable of moving each hind leg in the direction of the corresponding forehand on the same side.

The lateral exercises ridden on a single track described above, are listed in order of difficulty.

Principles of Single-Track Lateral Work

- The difficulty and sophistication of single-track lateral work should be tailored to the needs of each horse. When bending is minimal, the arc over which the horse is bent is large. The exercises become more sophisticated with increased lat-

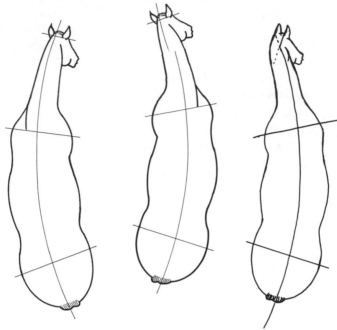

Patterns are not only gymnastically meaningless if ridden on a horse improperly bent but they can actually be detrimental. If one is riding a pattern on which a right-bending horse is necessary, it should look like the horse at left, the most important feature being a continuous and even bending of the spine! For horses, bending the supple neck is far easier than bending the lumbar back (cervical vs. lumbar spine).

The horse in the center is disengaging his outside hind leg by tilting his muzzle to the right (lowering his left ear) and pushing toward his right shoulder. By pivoting around his poll, he masterfully avoids engagement, which is work, and replaces it with lazy, gymnastically unproductive action. His neck is "broken" too because the spine behind the poll is pushed left, creating an S-curve in the spine. These many bodily evasions cause a loss of control over the haunches. It is like trying to write with a broken pencil. In horsemanship, the rider can only control a horse that remains connected from hock to muzzle. That presupposes an evenly bending and flexing spine.

Evasions produced by the horse on the right include an overflexion at the poll that could be as severe as going behind the bit. By doing this, he can virtually repeat all the other evasions seen in the horse in the center.

The horse can initiate these evasions and the rider must correct them. Even if they cannot successfully be corrected immediately, the rider, in time, ought to school the horse out of these severe faults. However, the troubles are compounded if these evasions are actually initiated by the rider. Pulling on the inside rein and not having the outside leg back, stretched (heel down) and draped on the horse, will force the horse to evade as shown.

eral bending throughout the horse's spine (and ribcage!). The development will be apparent and will manifest itself in the horse's increased suppleness and elasticity, which allows him to perform on smaller, tighter patterns.

- Easier and less sophisticated is the riding of fewer of these patterns (i.e., performing them once or twice rather than repeatedly) and in the case of serpentines, the riding of fewer and larger loops. Thus, difficulty of patterning always increases from large to small and from performing few or many repetitions.

- Enormously important is the principle of having to straighten the horse after each laterally bent pattern. Lateral bending must never be an enshrinement of eternally perpetuated lateral stiffness. A horse that is perpetually hollow to the right, for example, must be asked to straighten and then accept repositioning, followed by re-bending, before being allowed to proceed to the left on a pattern.

- In single-track lateral exercises, a correctly bending horse (if its conformation is suitable and its legs are not crooked) should "track" on a single track with each hind leg moving forward in the direction of the hoofprint of the front leg on the same side. Crossing over or stepping outward (straddling or sidestepping) with the hind legs, while performing circles and arcs, is indeed a serous fault, often unfortunately (for lack of time or awareness?) overlooked. Yet this concept is at the heart of gymnastic training and at the core of suppleness.

- The horse's entire spine and torso must be bent consistently throughout on the same continuous arc. An overpositioned neck, too much inward positioning of the head, haunches skidding outward or curved sharply inward, are all evasions of improving suppleness. In fact, they are the horse's ways of entrenching the status quo and reinforcing his existing stiffnesses rather than alleviating them. Rider-induced invitations to evade include overpositioning, manipulative hands that squeeze backwards on the horse's mouth to produce the illusion of softness and suppleness—also hands that steer the horse as if he were a bicycle. Using only one leg to suggest bending to the horse (usually the inside one) can cause another rider induced evasion. These are all wrong and produce illusionary "immediate" progress. The rider "feels" good things, but these are false feelings because he has "cheated" to produce them. The real issues remain untended to and uncorrected. The rider's equitational skills as well as his academic preparedness should demand that the horse remain under the influence of all the aids simultaneously (seat, both legs, and hands) thus producing the best continuous lateral bending interchangeable with appropriate episodes of utter straightness. This interchangeability of bending with straightness is one of the ways we have to critically assess true suppleness and the submission of the haunches to the rider's will.

- The horse's spine should always remain parallel to the pattern over which he moves. Lateral flexion on single-track patterns should not be postponed but rather should be pursued from the beginning of training—gradually, systematically and logically (and of course without force or compulsion). There is no neutrality in riding! We either contribute to the horse's well-being and development of his potentialities or we actively break him down. Horses that move incorrectly incur self-damage by the jarring impaction on the ground, which causes injuries—both small and large as well as both gradual or sudden—to the entire organism. All tissues from bone to muscle from ligament to sinew can and will be damaged by incorrect use. Only the rider can train for correct results and thereby safeguard his horse's well-being.

- The manege is a gymnasium and the logical patterns we ride in them carry the wisdom of centuries of training success. These classical patterns are training tools. All gymnasiums have equipment in them. Ours, the manege, is furnished only with the patterns the rider (trainer) knows to school his horse. The schooling patterns of our gymnasium become invested with meaning only when they are used by an academically prepared equestrian who is familiar with their rehabilitative, therapeutic and athletic uses. Beyond the effectiveness of patterns looms the mystery of their combinations. By combining patterns knowledgeably, their value increases geometrically.

Lateral work on a single track is infinite in its variety, but its basic elements are easy to recognize. The combinations can be likened to the infinite combinations that numbers can produce to make a telephone book. The only limits are the inventiveness and productive imagination of an enthusiastic rider.

LATERAL EXERCISE PATTERNS

A totally green horse, under the rider in the first few days of his training, will drift from side to side like a drunkard, staggering in and out of balance and seeking harmony with his new load. In such a case, the rider's wisdom should suggest that the horse be allowed to seek his own meandering path, over which the skilled rider must place his center of gravity as best he can. When the rider harmonizes with the horse's movement it helps the horse balance the combined weight package of horse and rider. The horse's confidence increases, as he becomes aware that his rider is harmonizing with his movements, and he will gradually listen to his rider's directions more willingly. Eventually, instead of just following the staggerings of the young horse, we can change his situation by using our now-familiar center of gravity to oppose his drifting. Now we can offer help not by accommodating him as before, but by suggesting to him a better way through an increased sophistication of his balance.

In order to "interfere" with the horse's drifting and begin to improve his balance, you will find it wise to turn him in the direction of his drifting shoulder. In other words, ride a large arc or circle in the direction toward which he is drifting. A young horse that hollows to the right and is drifting diagonally toward the left shoulder should be guided onto a left circle or arc. That will teach him to use his short-stepping and sometime-crossing left leg to support his motion. This will also help him "align" the left hind leg with the left front as the shoulder is moved inward on a turn. Eventually, the horse will discover how a little bending will absorb the shocks of strides and he will surrender to the will of the rider, not because he can "recognize the wisdom of it all" but because the motion will feel better to him.

When a young horse improves enough to obey our simple aids, we can begin to use patterns for suppling. These patterns can be described in groups. There are fundamental patterns or basic "models," and infinite elaborations of them can be devised. Modifications of patterns and varying their placement in the manege can make all the difference in whether we succeed in improving the horse or fail to benefit him.

The Hourglass Pattern

The hourglass pattern can be seen on the illustration (see page 79) by isolating the dotted diagonal lines and connecting them to the two half-circles at A and C. These combine into an hourglass that is one of the basic patterns of good gymnastic logic. This allows the lengthening of either the strides or the frame while straightening the horse on the two diagonals and collecting him at the short walls, while logically adding bending to facilitate collection naturally.

ELABORATIONS You may usefully elaborate to vary and improve results. Here are some possibilities:

1. Ride full circles at A and C before departing on the next diagonal. (See page 79.)
2. Diminish the size of the circles at A and C or keep them large, but precede them and follow them with deeply ridden, well-bent corners for added sophistication in collection and bending.
3. The serpentine in three loops can be intermixed with or added to the original pattern to avoid anticipation, create interest and monitor the level of suspension, balance and rhythm as the work progresses.
4. Make the serpentine perpetual by continuously riding one from A to C and back. As earlier noted, one can "suspend" the serpentine to pursue a circle, especially toward the stiff side of the horse (usually the left).
5. Mix serpentines and circles and finally return to adding the occasional extension on a diagonal to check if you can still straighten your horse and ride him forward—thus through

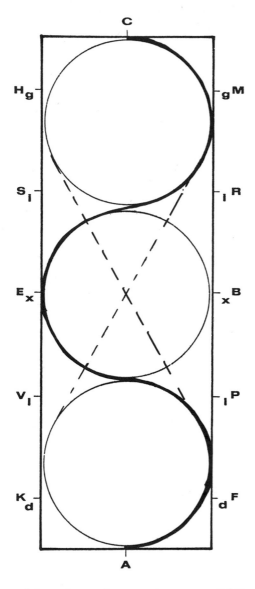

elaborations, the exercise comes "full circle" to the original, fundamental purpose of the hourglass pattern.

Short Diagonals

The exercises illustrated in the illustration on page 80 are based on riding short diagonals. To illustrate short diagonals, imagine connections between M and E, or R and V, or B and K. Doing the same on the other side of the arena, you can get three more short diagonals. The simple basic pattern consists of riding any short diagonal, testing your ability in bending your horse and then straightening him. You always have the option of extending the strides or the frame on the straight parts of the pattern and collecting on the arcs and circles.

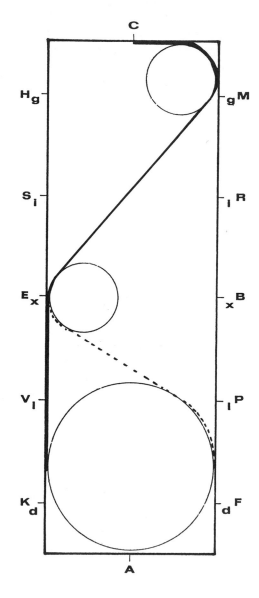

THE ATHLETIC DEVELOPMENT OF THE DRESSAGE HORSE

ELABORATIONS   Here are some variations to try:

1. Ride two short diagonals by following an M to E to F pattern and repeat on the other side by riding from K to B to H.
2. Ride circles of any size appropriate (to the horse's development) after each short diagonal. When opting to ride a 20m circle in this combination, you can attempt to retain the extension created on the diagonal.
3. The dotted line in the diagram on page 80 illustrates one way to incorporate a change of rein pattern and also shows how to shape larger and smaller circles smoothly. The variety of possibilities is enormous. Mostly they are not illustrated here, but by looking at the 8m and 10m circles, you will discover that there is a set of exercises where you can proceed straight along the walls of the manege and down the center line, straightening and extending your horse, yet bending and collecting him by riding each corner as a part of a circle! The size of the circle in the corners should depend on the development of the horse. Also, circles can be introduced as an elaboration on this basic pattern by riding one at each letter you pass.
4. Sets of circles can be ridden as shown in the illustration on page 82. For example, the thick line on the left side, traveling from C to H to X to K to A is a simple serpentine. This is a fine exercise for balancing the horse and making him attentive, and it is an indispensable method of straightening the horse that travels crooked in extended trot.

Elaborations should include:

1. Periodic insertions of circles.
2. The pattern that starts at F and returns to B on the right rein serves as a reminder that counter patterns should be used often.
3. The simple serpentine can be revisited by looping it around in many inventive ways. This includes using the three smaller circles shown and the option of riding along either the inner or outer perimeter of the center circle at E.

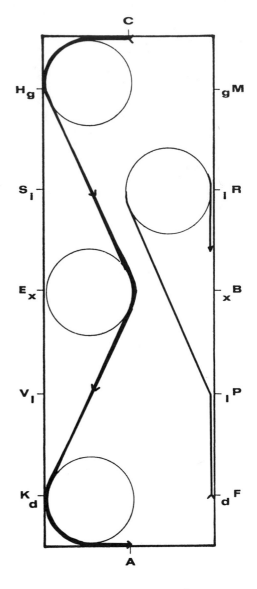

Remember that these patterns are suggestions and not meant to be a cure-all. In fact, any and all patterns discussed here or elsewhere can weigh in equally as therapeutically wonderful or as dreadfully destructive, depending upon who applies them, how they are applied and when they are applied. Appropriateness cannot be learned from a book. This is why there is no "recipe book for riding" and why riding remains eternally a coached art! As with all art, the art of riding is based on apprenticeship and daily interaction—never exclusively on reading. Yet, without an understanding of theory, a rider is simply not coachable.

THE ALIGNMENT OF THE HAUNCHES WITH THE SHOULDERS

Schooling horses demands from the rider the academic understanding and the physical feel and the skills to "place" the horse's haunches wherever the rider wants to and to do the same with the forehand (shoulders). The relative placement of haunches and shoulders to each other is very important. Our success in straightening the horse and riding it forward depends heavily on this skill.

For this reason the serpentine is a very important exercise and one of the most difficult. During any serpentine the relative travel and displacement of haunches and shoulders change almost from stride to stride. It is worth recalling again that each corner of the manege is a portion of a circle and also a potential portion of a serpentine.

Serpentines for Improvement and Correction

During serpentines one can experiment with changing gaits to the walk (from the trot or canter) before changing the horse's lateral bend on a serpentine. The walk is the only gait without suspension and therefore the horse can be best controlled at the walk. The transitions to the walk help secure the half-halts which help re-balance the horse's weight toward the haunches. Such transition work is equally beneficial for making improvements on figure-8 patterns.

ELABORATIONS Serpentines performed at the canter can remain on the same lead, alternating each loop between a true canter and a counter canter. Or one can insist on transitions to either the trot or the walk when changing direction and bending. With advanced horses one can perform a flying change to change direction and bending at the moment of the lead change.

Nine

Ways to Increase Suspension

Now that we have discussed the fundamental patterns that can be done on single tracks, we must take a moment to emphasize the importance of suspension in the trot and in the canter. All too often riders become victims of a strategy that pursues the attainment of form without the proper content. Actually, impeccable content defines the magnificent form of any art, including the art of horsemanship. Those who pursue "imitation" dressage do so because of a lack of academic preparation. Riding must first be understood before it can be practiced.

There are many components to correct content in equitation, but none is more important than the creation of enough activity in the haunches to sustain the necessary suspension in the trot and canter. Without the proper articulation and powerful engagement of the joints, there will not be enough suspension in the strides. We must remember that it is not sufficient to let the horse move forward, but rather we must ask him to *carry* forward. The lifting action is at the heart of proper forward locomotion. Therefore, we ought to insist in our gymnasticizing that the horse move "forward upward."

The definitive features of both the trot and canter include

a period of suspension, during which none of the horse's legs touch the ground. The total lack of impaction is supplanted by forward flight over space suspended above the ground. The finest athletic achievement for the horse includes the skill of carrying a rider powerfully during sustained suspension. Thus, the horse should progress with his rider in flight, rather than by crawling on the ground. The latter often-seen but despicable training result includes putting the horse on his forehand, where he dwells after impacting the ground. A correctly schooled horse will travel ever so briefly over his forehand but will not spend time dwelling on it with his weight.

Here are some exercises that will help to increase a horse's suspension:

Exercise 1

Alternate between powerfully lengthening strides and collecting to shorter but higher strides. We all know that the ultimate result of correct schooling must be a horse that can collect and extend his gait in the exact same rhythm. Right now the fashion tends to favor speed, so that we see the same rhythm in both extension and collection as being excessively rapid. Instead, a well-suspended horse in correct carriage and engaged over his haunches will show the tendency to deliver the extended trot like the longest possible passage: enormous suspension in slow motion while the ultimate length of stride is attained. The slower both extension and collection are in rhythm, the more likely they are to be engaged, seated, and liberated off the forehand. Moving "uphill" and with suspension proves self-carriage.

However, beginnings are not identical to final perfection. Every perfect movement has a long history of imperfections behind it. The means to a goal can never be identical to the goal. Thus, when beginning this exercise, we must make allowances for the horse to "speed up," as little as possible, when asked to extend. Similarly, when asked to collect we must allow him to slow his rhythm, for he is not yet elastic enough to render these severe transitions in impeccable balance and rhythm. In fact, the "collection" at first should resemble an attempted, but never

Arthur Kottas-Heldenberg, Chief Rider of the Spanish Riding School, is schooling a warmblood. Everything one ought to emulate is shown in these three photographs. When a rider sits and aids as he does, the rider simply becomes superbly elegant by inevitability. The correct contents always define the exceptionally beautiful form.

Opposite above, the horse is at a medium trot and below, in a passage. He is extending the trot in the photograph above. These pictures reveal the most important goals of dressage, which are to perfect the natural gaits by "magnifying" them. All three pictures show optimum engagement, elastic articulation of the joints, energy blanketing a "liquid"-looking horse whose energy is limitless. The horse moves in his entirety. Through the haunches and the swinging loose, articulating back, the horse's energies travel to light, elevated, free forehands. The withers dance high, the horse's elbows are free and the shoulders rotate, allowing the forearms to reach fully forward and upward. Clearly the photographs opposite below and above illustrate the emphasis that whether we collect or extend we maximize motion, either toward vertical or toward horizontal engagement. The extended trot looks like the longest passage and the passage looks like the tallest extension. The horse goes through his neck and arrives at a comfortable, wet mouth that senses the rider's mind, not his hands.

In all three pictures both the musculature and the skeletal functions are absolutely correct.

The specific purpose of "pattern illustration" here is to emphasize that the medium trot is the essential gait for the development of higher-level gymnastic engagement. Out of that strong athletic gait comes the passage and extension. Both gaits are analogous to the two branches of the letter Y sharing a common stem, which represents the medium trot. Photos: Andreas Jarc.

completed, transition toward walk. One must bring the horse from a trot to the brink of a walk but never lose the trot. When the horse becomes more advanced this exercise can also be done in the canter. This, incidentally, tests the rider's equitational skill in maintaining driving while sustaining the forehand, the very essence of any good half-halt. In this exercise, as soon as the horse answers the call to collection by slowing and preparing a transition, we ask him to move powerfully forward to lengthened strides.

The exercise becomes more sophisticated when the rider can alternate between longer and shorter strides very frequently, within few steps, and when the collections lose their "doggieness" and the extensions lose their rushing. In short, as the rhythm becomes more dependably even and the changes between shorter and longer strides become smoother, we arrive at our ideal. In doing these exercises horses will inevitably become much more active with the haunches (especially at the hocks) and will begin to lift their rider higher as progress strengthens their quarters.

Exercise 2

Another exercise that improves suspension depends on lengthening the reins gradually (even to the buckle) while driving forward to lengthening strides. As soon as the rein reaches its ultimate length and the horse's neck is stretched forward and down, we must gather the contact gently and tactfully. Here, we omit the collecting or slowing of the strides. All work is done while lengthening the stride because we only change the length and position of the topline.

The purpose of this exercise is to elevate the horse's back and induce the lumbar back to flex more. As soon as the horse's back swings more and increases its articulation, the horse can improve his carriage and suspension. In fact, suspension depends most essentially on the freedom of the horse's back to articulate supply under his rider. The strength of many muscle systems and the very skill of pushing the back up, tilting the hips forward and rounding the lumbar area ultimately makes suspension possible. Horses that lack suspension and run like rodents on an attic floor certainly testify to having stiff, immobile, inarticulate and hard backs. Surely they are hurting and also deliver a tough ride to the rider, who perhaps deserves it.

Exercise 3

This exercise to create and then improve suspension involves repeated transitions between the trot and canter. While performing these frequent transitions, we must only encourage lengthened strides in the trot and the rider should be rising, and we must attempt slow collected strides in the canter. With this exercise we again contribute greatly to the loosening and articulation of the horse's back. The trot-canter and canter-trot transitions are the very exercises that are most successful for mobilizing the horse's back. However, Exercise 2 is most valuable and appropriate for elevating the horse's back.

Suspension will grow both in the trot and in the canter. The secret resides in using the natural energy generated by cantering, in the trot. Conversely, we can collect the canter more easily because the horse will seek "repose" after the aggressively driven trot. One must feel confident that even the energetic trot, which frequently follows a session of canter, can and should be driven.

Ten

Lateral Bending
On Two Tracks

Whenever we discuss horses that bend laterally and progress on curved patterns, we use a terminology that refers to the "inside" and "outside" of the horse. Originally the "inside of the horse" was simply the one visible from the center of the manege, and his "outside" was the one facing the wall. Usually a horse is asked to bend, more acutely or less so, toward the inside. This requirement is necessitated by the horse having to place his center of gravity to the inner side of his spine and activate his inside hind leg more to act as a shock absorber in curves and corners. Even along a straight wall, progressing straight forward, we create a "functionally" rather than a "geometrically" straight horse. The functionally straight horse is ridden to align his inside shoulder exactly in front of his inside hip. The hips being wider than the shoulders requires that the horse move with an ever so slight inward positioning while progressing along a straight path. Seldom must one ride the horse ruler-straight. However, one may do so often when riding in open country. In a manege, only on diagonals and on paths parallel to, but away from the walls do we ride the horse ruler-straight. Examples of the latter are quarter, three-quarter, center line, half-arena line and inside track. But let us return to straightening the horse along the walls of the manege and riding him over the many and frequently required bent lines and we will find that the horse needs to be minimally positioned but evenly bent toward the inside of the arena.

The terminology, however, needs further explanation because we often need to ride counter patterns in contrast to patterns moving inward from the wall with an inward-bending horse. On counter patterns, including those ridden in a counter canter, we must bend the horse in the opposite direction from the pattern over which he moves. Counter patterns and counter-bending horses, absolutely essential to reaching the ideal gymnastic goals, are mostly absent from competition tests, with the notable exception of the counter canter. Competition tests are vehicles for evaluating the horse's progress. Judges can best evaluate the horse's accomplishments when he is asked to show the ideals toward which we hope to progress. Judges are not well served by viewing "means toward ideals." Those are training devices and eminently necessary ones, for one never reaches a goal without the appropriate, however different, means that lead to it. Consequently even the eternally predominating goal of "straighten your horse and ride him forward" is accomplished with the frequent assistance of curved patterns and bent horses. Straightness is made possible by lateral flexibility, just as collection is made possible by extensions, and indeed extensions improve by advancing collection!

During a performance of a counter pattern, then, the horse must be evenly bent in the direction opposite to the one in which he is progressing. Yet when a horse is moving on a true 20m circle, we expect him to be "properly" bent inward, his spine paralleling the exact arc of the circle. However, on a circle ridden with counter flexion, the horse will be asked to hollow toward the wall and bend away from the center of the circle.

Here is the essence of my explanation, without which my description of patterns would be impossible to understand and follow. Regardless of which way our horse is bent while moving on circle, we must always define as his inside, and the rider's inside the side that is hollow and toward which the horse is laterally bent. For instance, a horse in a true canter on the left

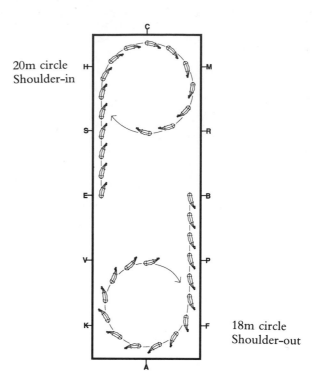

20m circle
Shoulder-in

18m circle
Shoulder-out

This illustration shows a highly sophisticated way of schooling in true patterns and counter patterns. The shoulder-in is being demonstrated.

This most important of two-track suppling exercises can be done along a straight line (here a wall) or on a 20m circle. The demand on both horse and rider sharply increases when the shoulder-in is progressing on a circle. For on a circle we do not have the security of the wall to help us know we have the correct (about 33 degrees) angulation inward from haunches to shoulder, and it is more difficult to feel the continuum and evenness of the horse's bending.

The demand, and with it the gymnastic value, increases when the shoulder-out is performed. Then the major difference is that the horse's "outside shoulder," now physically to the inside from the wall, is easier to monitor and control. Also, the horse's body strengthens by moving the weight more toward the leading (in this illustration the right) shoulder.

When doing a shoulder-out on the circle, one ought to decrease the diameter to 18m to allow enough "clearance" for the horse's head and neck. Thus when his haunches track on an 18m circle, the head is still out on a 20m circle. At the shoulder-out the horse cannot so easily evade crossing and especially forward support with the "inside hind leg" as he possibly can during a shoulder-in. The shoulder-out, by virtue of the pattern's progression, defines for the horse more properly where his activated inside hind leg (here the left) should print to maximize its articulation and focus on weight bearing.

Diagram: Barbara Leistico.

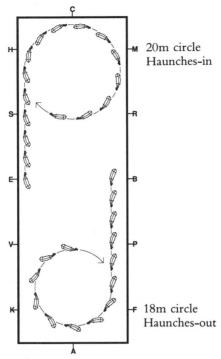

20m circle
Haunches-in

18m circle
Haunches-out

The haunches-in is more difficult for the horse than the shoulder-in. Here we see the same patterns as we saw before but done with the horse performing the haunches-in and the haunches-out. A great deal more strengthing issues from these than from the shoulder-in, which supples more. The control of the haunches is synonymous with the goals of all dressage. If a rider succeeds in controlling the haunches-in, without diminishing the purity and brilliance of the gait in which it is practiced, great gymnastic successes can follow. The haunches-in and the haunches-out can be practiced in all three gaits, the walk, trot and canter. However, I most emphatically advise not to do haunches-in at the canter, as that is a natural evasion maneuver of the horse that hopes to avoid working under and forward properly with the inside hind leg. Here it is wise to remember that most exercises that we ask the horse to do, he would also do as a disobedience by himself.

What is the difference between a deliberate counter canter and being on the wrong lead? What is the difference between a crooked canter and a haunches-in? What is the difference between a horse drifting back from a halt or a rein-back? A lot. Only when the rider initiates and defines the quality of the movement by control toward collection is the movement valid. Otherwise, horse-initiated and lacking in collection, the movements are merely disobediences with no gymnastic value!

The haunches-out, especially ridden on a 20m circle, is very valuable as a counter-canter exercise. It is one of the most effective ways to increase control with regard to collection of the haunches during canter. While the horse can evade engagement during a haunches-in at the canter and will volunteer it precisely to evade straightness, at the haunches-out in counter-canter he must "sit down" and engage. He will increase his lumbar articulation and increase his pelvic tuck. He will tax very much his hips and increase his collection, almost to the degree such is demanded during a pirouette. In fact, a clever rider, after proper time for preparation, will do pirouette work from haunches-out on a circle at the time the horse is about on the center line. You can add that to this illustration with your imagination: Pirouette your horse to the left (where he is bending already) when crossing the center line.   Diagram: Barbara Leistico.

lead, proceeding left on a circle has his inside on the left, toward which he is bent. On this side the muscles are contracted and the inside hind leg performs with greater articulation. Now the same horse on a left circle but moving on the right lead, performing a counter canter, will have his inside to the right! While that is on the outside toward the wall, we still call it his inside. That is because he is hollow toward his right side and he is bent to the right. The right is the side on which his muscles are contracted.

This principle of the inside always being the side toward which the horse is bending applies to the rider as well. When referring to the rider's inside seatbone or hand or leg position, we mean the one toward which the horse is bent and not necessarily the one nearest the center of the manege.

In short, inside is toward the hollow, shorter side of the horse, regardless of where the walls of the manege happen to be relative to our motion. Coincidentally, the inside is usually toward the inside of the manege because we usually train on true patterns and less often on counter patterns.

AN OVERVIEW OF THE TWO-TRACK MOVEMENTS
The Leg-Yield

The leg-yield is a sideways movement by the horse as he responds to his rider's unilateral (one-sided) leg pressure. Yielding away from leg pressure is contrary to the horse's instinctually coded responses. Horses are instinctively claustrophobic animals and when enclosed, confined, tied down or in any way hemmed in they instinctively want to and sometimes actually do break out. They respond, usually and most naturally, by pushing or pulling against pressure. One example of this instinct-derivative behavior is when the horse pulls on reins that are tightly held. When riders complain to me about their horses pulling their arm out of its socket, I reply that the horse just reported that his mouth is being pulled. Usually horses and riders pull harder on the left rein. As anyone knows who has been in rope-pulling contests, it takes two to pull. High hands will generate the same instinct and bring the horse's poll (not, unfortunately, the middle of the neck) too low and set him behind the bit.

To teach the horse an entire language of controls based on his moving *away from leg pressure* rather than leaning into the pressure, against the rider's leg, is a difficult and often delicate matter. Instinct tells the horse to push against the rider's leg and the more stiffly a leg is used by the rider, the more aggressive it seems to the horse, thus urging him all the more to lean against it and not move away from it as we hope to teach him to do. To our advantage there is a group of muscles along the horse's sides located exactly where a *correctly placed* rider's calf should be stretched and wrapped around the horse's barrel. By lightly and rhythmically stimulating these muscles in this location, the sympathetic muscle groups in the horse's haunches react by contracting, thus causing increased activity in the haunches. The rider's correctly placed legs, applying the right kind and amount of stimuli, will cause the horse to become active and enable him to move away from the driving leg contrary to instinct.

That is why we teach the leg-yield. We must communicate the difficult but singularly important lesson to the horse that our leg pressure is asking for motion away from it and increased activity in the haunches. In general, once this lesson is learned, the habits of the horse are gradually formed so that he no longer hesitates to move away from our leg pressure. The leg-yield, having served its purpose, loses its importance.

The leg-yield is of no rehabilitative, therapeutic or athletic value to the horse, whatsoever. In fact, one could easily argue that it can cause harmfully counterproductive stiffening and disengagement. This is a high price to pay for teaching a horse to re-balance sideways and obey the rider's leg pressure. These requirements can be better taught and schooled through more athletically useful exercises, such as the shoulder-in.

The Shoulder-in

The most important, most fundamental and relatively "recent" gymnastic exercises is the shoulder-in, which was introduced just over two hundred years ago. As with all two-track or other gymnastically valid exercises, the shoulder-in addresses a favorable development of the entire horse. Body building, complex balancing sideways, increased elasticity in the use of muscles,

This illustration shows a horse at a shoulder-in. Yet he could as well be a horse commencing a 10m circle. Here I want to show that in all lateral bending exercises, regardless of whether the horse is moving on two tracks (shoulder-in) or a circle (arc), one must be absolutely sure that his spine, and consequently his torso, is evenly bent. The lightly muscled, long, willowy, dangling, elastic and nimble neck will always offer to bend more than the much more rigid, thick, barrel-like torso will. The art is to unite the horse into one continuous "bow" and forbid him the evasion by overpositioning his neck, thereby preventing a straight, stiff torso.

Notice that the horse's hips must remain perpendicularly lined up with

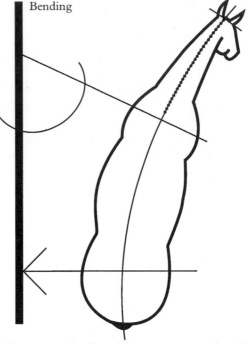

Bending

the wall along which he travels in a shoulder-in. His shoulders, however, are inward at 33 degrees. If the shoulders are allowed to stay closer to the wall, the horse is too straight to engage enough to strengthen and supple. If he is "overangled" and his shoulders are brought in too far, he loses his bend and he can also evade all engagement and cross feet shallow, as in a leg-yield, destroying the meaning and gymnastic value of a shoulder-in.

To perform any bent movement with precision, the rider must remain in perfect control of the horse's shoulders (forehand). That control must be at the withers, the base of the neck. Riders who pull the horse's head and neck inward with the inside rein will address the outer end of the neck and contribute to the possibility of evasion by overbending at the neck or tilting the head (one ear lower and muzzle to one side). These troubles caused by the overuse of inside rein are also inhibiting to the forward thrust of the inside hind leg—the very limb that is supposed to increase its weight bearing and articulation on the circle and also during the shoulder-in. The enemy of bending is the ill-used inside rein! Riders with a wide hand position, as though holding the handle bars of a bicycle and steering about the horse's face, cannot gymnasticize and supple a horse. Good hands are next to one another, holding even reins (never shorten the inside), and make the horse feel as if all reins are always held in one fist. Only we should know that we are holding the reins in two hands, the horse should not. This will allow him to bend from the rider's legs between reins that feel like the eye of a needle through which the horse's neck is threaded.

Diagram: Barbara Leistico.

strengthening, therefore suppling, of the joints and so on are all results of shoulder-in work. However, this exercise's most potent contributions are (1) the strengthening of the inside hock, which is asked to articulate higher and yet more forward than when not in a shoulder-in. It has high collection value because it engages forward and upward to magnify the strides. Concurrent with increased hock articulation is an ability to lower the hip on the inside and contribute to an increased contraction of the torso's muscles along the inside while stretching those along the outside. The back muscles along the outside of the spine are always rounded and pushed up higher during a shoulder-in. And (2) the limbering of the shoulders is another great result of shoulder-in exercises. While the inside front leg of the horse must "merely cross" rather than "straddle," the shoulders loosen significantly. Crossing means that the horse's inside foreleg prints on the ground just in front of the outside front hoof but not past it, as opposed to straddling past the outside front hoofprint. The loosening of the shoulder area contributes to the horse's ability to elevate the forehand when properly engaged. Elevating the forehand means the "bouncing" of the withers higher, and coincidentally allowing the neck to arch higher with the poll carried at the highest position developmentally possible at the time.

The shoulder-out is simply a shoulder-in movement that is performed on a counter pattern. The shoulder-in is performed with an inward bending horse and is unique among all two-track movements in that while bending inward, the horse moves "outward" away from the direction of his body curvature. The shoulder-in left is performed by a left-bending horse that moves toward the direction of the right shoulder. Progression is toward the right, yet bending is toward the left.

In the corresponding shoulder-out, the horse is bent to the left and still progresses to the right. Then what is the difference and why is the shoulder-out a counter pattern? Because it is performed against the direction of progression. A shoulder-out left is done by a horse along the wall of the manege, bending left, head toward the wall but progressing along it toward his right shoulder. When done on a 20m circle, where this exercise is the most useful, the horse performing shoulder-out left will

The shoulder-in, and it could not be better! Everything that defines a shoulder-in is here. Notice the rider's "stretched and draped," motionless, "adhesive" leg position, which effortlessly and inevitably presents a deep heel, shock-absorbing ankles and perpetual contact from the seat downward to the ankles. Neither horse nor rider stress or strain. The wonderful neck, which is controlled at the "base" (withers) and not at the mouth, with even ears and a vertically hanging head, speaks for the activity in the haunches, the continuum of lateral bending and the grand posture created by the lengthening of the forehand. The rider is Arthur Kottas-Heldenberg, Chief Rider of the Spanish Riding School.   Photo: Andreas Jarc.

be moving on a circle to the right, bending to the left and counter to the arc of the circle. During a shoulder-out the horse is still more articulate on his inside hind leg (in this example the left) but his weight-bearing shifts to the outside hind leg (the right) as it is tracking toward the direction of the circle's (or the manege's) center.

The shoulder-in and shoulder-out can be done at the walk and at the trot. The walk might teach the horse how best to deliver it and the rider, if needed, how best to control it. However, its most athletic usefulness occurs when done at the trot.

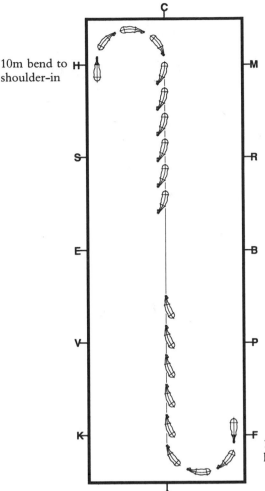

C

10m bend to shoulder-in H

M

S

R

E

B

V

P

K

F

10m bend to haunches-in

A

The 10m half-circle and the horse's proper bending on it is an excellent beginning to both the shoulder-in and the haunches-in. I placed both movements on the center line in this illustration because this gives the proper preparation. But also, more importantly, it shows that with your imagination you can place an "invisible wall" at the center line next to the horse's "outside," which is his long side. That way we see the shoulder-in and the haunches-in.

However, if in your imagination you place an "invisible wall" along the horse "inside," toward which he is bent, you can see the shoulder-out and the haunches-out. In short, the shoulder-in right you see illustrated here can also be the shoulder-out left, depending on along which wall, real or imaginary, it is performed! The haunches-in right is simultaneously a haunches-out left. The terminology merely changes (but not the movement of the horse) to designate the horse's progression relative to a wall. Diagram: Barbara Leistico.

Without the suspension and impulsion of the trot, the articulation of the inside hock, and the strengthening of lateral balancing, the elevation of the forehand would not be as easily forthcoming.

The Plié

The plié resembles a shoulder-in exercise. In the canter a horse cannot do a shoulder-in because he is not permitted to cross his inside legs in front of his outside legs, in order to avoid damage

The plié engages the horse's inside hind leg more, and contributes collection, when done without a diagonal drifting. While pliés on diagonals are the necessary beginnings, later the horse can perform a shoulder-fore along a 20m circle or along the wall. The inside shoulder of the horse should be placed directly in front of his inside hip. The rider must never pull on the inside rein and inhibit the very inside leg he is trying to engage. Instead, as always, the shoulders ought to be controlled inward by both hands, mainly the outside one, and allow the horse to volunteer a mild neck bending, which he inevitably does to balance himself. The rider must always ride the "base of the neck" of the horse and never "steer" the outer end of it, which is the mouth. Twisting the horse's face to one side is the very dismantling of the rider's influences over the whereabouts of the haunches.

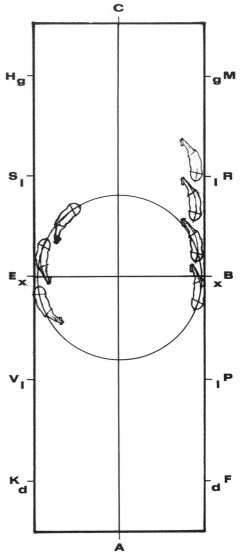

and stress. However, one may do a diagonal movement across part of the manege, "drifting" toward the outside shoulder, with bending increased to the inside and the inside hind leg keenly engaged. This is the key to beginning collection at the canter for many horses. As a result of increased engagement through sideways movement "outward," away from the direction of bending, the horse will assume more weight in the haunches (collection) and engage more on the inside hock.

When done along a straight line such as the wall or center line, this exercise is called the shoulder-fore. It is more akin to the shoulder-in than the plié, which is by virtue of patterning similarities more akin to a leg-yield. The shoulder-fore moves along patterns that are used in the shoulder-in. The horse is asked to bring his inside shoulder just in front of or slightly to the inside of his inside hip bone but not exaggerating enough to necessitate crossing with the inside hind leg. As the horse's shoulder is brought inward and placed in front of the inside hip, he can no longer evade collection by possibly pushing inward with his haunches. This is a common evasion because it allows the horse to continue with his canter without engaging his hocks. With the shoulder-fore his inside hock must assume the weight-bearing responsibilities, having been properly lined up with the forehand on the inner side. This will cause the necessary articulation for the inside hock required to promote collection.

COMPARING AND CONTRASTING THE SHOULDER-IN WITH THE LEG-YIELD

Often I am asked why I think so highly of shoulder-in exercises but find the leg-yield of little use. There is also much debate about the precise requirements for shoulder-in, especially whether it should be performed on three or four tracks.

A good way to analyze the differences between the shoulder-in and leg-yield is to think of these movements in terms of their components. The shoulder-in is well described in many books, especially in the *Ecole de Cavalerie*, written by François Robichon de la Guérinière more than two hundred fifty years ago. It is described for contemporaries in the FEI's *Rules for Dressage Events*. De la Guérinière discovered and introduced the shoulder-in. He considered this movement the alpha and omega of all suppling and collection exercises. Today the FEI protects the integrity of the exercise and gives guidelines for maintaining the standard for evaluating it when performed.

In these pictures Susan Derr Drake is riding Will Power. Left, she does a shoulder-in to the left at the trot. Notice how her outside leg remains slightly behind the invisible inside leg, as it always should whenever we bend a horse. The outside leg's back position insures bending and guards the haunches from slipping, swinging outward, and guarantees that the shoulder-in does not turn into a "running away sideways" from the inside leg in an uncontrolled drift, but rather that by bending a gymnastically valid and valuable exercise develops. Her continuous bending of the horse, control of the forehand at the base of the neck, where it should be, makes the movement correct.

Center, Susan Derr Drake rides a leg-yield to the right. Ideally the leg-yield should present a straight horse. Mostly and unfortunately, we see horses "counterflexing" by hollowing toward the leg of displacement, away from the direction of movement. In these pictures, however, you see the movement as it should be: a straight horse with crossing legs. Again, the rider's art in coordinating for the horse the interplay between haunches and forehand is the key to success. The forehand is controlled enough not to "lead off with a bulge" at the shoulder. Notice especially how in the picture on the right the horse crosses with the hind legs and in the center one, with the forehands. Seldom can you see such a correct, balanced, active leg-yield as in these photographs. That is why there is already a hint from the horse that the future half-pass will come easily.

Photos: Paul Drake.

In a good shoulder-in the horse should move along the wall or straight lines parallel to it at a 33-degree angle, which, for most horses, is the angulation that allows continuous and even bending around the rider's inside leg. An imaginary line connecting the base of the horse's tail to his withers and the line along which he moves should form the 33-degree angle. However, the haunches remain tracking along the wall, or whatever the original path of travel was. A line drawn through the horse's hips should remain at right angles to the wall.

The horse should stride with his inside hind leg, not merely in front of his outside hind hoofprint but well forward and under in the direction of the hoofprint left by his outside forehand. The length and unencumbered reach of the inside hind leg is one of the most important features of this exercise. This exercise is primarily for the strengthening of the inside hind leg, particularly the hock. Strength and suppleness are synonymous with the horse's gymnastic development of his joints. The shoulders are liberated and limbered, as the horse is expected to cross with his inside foreleg in front of the outside foreleg but not to straddle with it past the outside front leg. The proper crossing of the legs depends entirely on the rider's ability to create and maintain a continuous and even lateral bending in the horse and his ability to maintain impulsion in the original rhythm. If suspension in the trot diminishes, the impulsion is already insufficient and the horse should not "drop to the floor" and lose his cadence just because he is asked to perform a shoulder-in.

One of the paramount gymnastic goals remains the magnification or amplification of the basic gaits while retaining their pure form. If the shoulder-in becomes overangled by bringing the shoulders more than 33 degrees away from the wall, the strides inevitably become stiff, mincing and choppy, and cross but without reaching forward. The ground-gaining qualities as well as the cadenced elevation will be compromised. Equally detrimental is the overbending of the neck relative to the rest of the body. This allows the horse to "escape" through his outside shoulder and produce a "head-in" or "neck-in," which has no benefit but to teach the horse a dangerous evasion to bending. This mistake is caused by riders pulling on the inside rein. Their illusion is of a well-bending horse as they pull the horse's neck toward their inside kneecap, and with this harsh inside rein they prevent any possible engagement of the horse's inside hind leg. In fact, the inside hind leg is inhibited and cannot move either sideways or forward, nor articulate upward properly. The inside rein's pulling will actually destroy the shoulder-in.

Ideally, a fully gymnasticized, truly supple horse will deliver a shoulder-in on three tracks. One track of footprints will be described by his outside hind leg, the second by the outside foreleg with the inside hind leg traveling exactly aligned on the same path and the third by the inside front leg.

However, before all these ideal elements are in place, one must often allow horses to execute a shoulder-in on four tracks. Care should be taken that the four tracks are not due to the haunches drifting too far out with the torso straightening. That produces a leg-yield and annihilates the shoulder-in. Riding on four tracks with younger horses diminishes the importance of collection and teaches the following skills: crossing the legs to

Susan Derr Drake on Will Power is riding a shoulder-in. Notice the excellent alignment of the legs of both the rider and the horse. The good leg position of the rider determines the good tracking of the horse. Here Will Power leaves three tracks of hoofprints in the sand. That is the ideal to which we must aspire when developing the shoulder-in. Advanced horses, already performing good collection, are expected to do exactly that: perform a shoulder-in on three tracks, yet with proper bending and inside hind leg engaging not only inward but forward, well under the center of gravity. Here these elements are obvious.

Photo: Paul Drake.

travel sideways and displacing the center of gravity outward, in a direction opposite from that of the bend. Horses must be schooled literally step by step in these complex movements. After all, they have wonderful memories but no complex conceptualization. Once horses understand and develop the skills of moving sideways with properly crossing legs, one can actually increase the collection with half-halts as well as with tempo changes. Then one can introduce the alternating demands of extending and collecting the strides while in a shoulder-in to produce the desired flexibility, suppleness and strength. Eventually the horse will voluntarily perform the "finished," or ideal, shoulder-in with all its elements in place, including moving on three tracks rather than four.

It is essential to understand that the ideal will result from schooling all of the elements correctly: angulation from the wall, consistency of lateral bending, degree of crossing, degree of the forward reach of steps and degree of cadenced elevation.

THE HAUNCHES-IN AND THE HAUNCHES-OUT

The haunches-in is a very sophisticated exercise. It requires the horse's crossing his outside hind leg in front of the inside one while perfectly and evenly bending inward in the direction of actual progression. The exercise puts a great deal of stress on the stifles, especially the inside one. The hips experience stress also, especially the outside hip but somewhat less than the stifles. Because the haunches-in is a strengthening exercise, it is simultaneously a suppling exercise for the stifles and hips. The weight-bearing is more on the inside hind leg, which accounts for the stifle stress there. However, the sinking-reaching articulation is greater with the outside hind leg which is why it is valuable for the outside hip. The lumbar back, which is crucial to all gymnastic development in the horse, gets a powerful lesson in "articulation" both in vertical "swinging" and in lateral "rocking." It is a most difficult exercise for the horse to properly execute with ease, which is why one sees all too few done well. Usually the lateral bending is missing and the suspension and cadence are compromised as the weak, stressed horse signals his fatigue or discomfort by "flatly falling to the ground" in his trot.

This exercise can best be taught at the walk, but its gymnastic value comes with the trot. Haunches-in can also be performed at the canter, but I am against it. Horses tend to use haunches-inward in the canter as an evasion: the inside hind leg is being saved or allowed to remain stiff. This prevents collection and engagement from developing and violates the eternal admonition to "straighten your horse and ride him forward." All haunches-inward evasions at the canter should be strictly pro-

Elizabeth Ball is asking her horse, Bolshoj, to perform the haunches-in right at the walk. Some of the important components of this most difficult movement are easily observed. The horse is bent evenly to the right but positioned along the wall in such a manner as to allow the neck to proceed straight, parallel with the wall, and only from the withers back is the horse's right bending allowed to curve away from the wall. Often one sees the fault that the horse's haunches are in but so are his head and neck pulled in. That pushes his outside shoulder to the wall and coils both front and back inward from that leaning shoulder. As you see, Elizabeth Ball's riding does not show such a mistake but is correctly proceeding along the wall. Notice also that the haunches-in must always progress on four tracks. Remember that the ideal shoulder-in is to proceed on only three tracks, the inside hind and outside foreleg proceeding on an identical path. Not so in haunches-in, where only progressing on four track assures us of the sufficient lumbar bending of the horse when the neck is kept parallel to the line of progression.

Photo: Richard F. Williams.

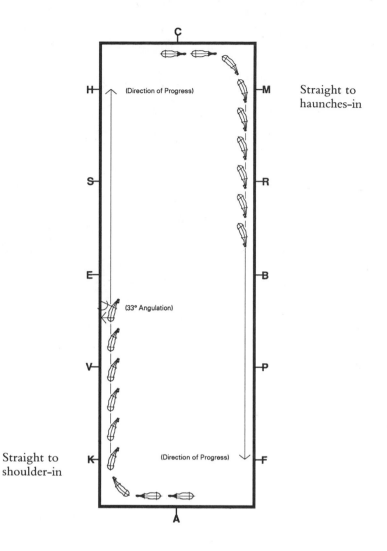

Diagram labels:
- C
- Straight to haunches-in
- (Direction of Progress)
- H — M
- S — R
- E — B
- (33° Angulation)
- V — P
- Straight to shoulder-in
- K — F
- (Direction of Progress)
- A

While earlier you saw the same two movements, the shoulder-in and the shoulder-out, on the center line, now we view shoulder-in along the wall. The haunches-in is illustrated in this location by the rider in the preceding photograph. Here only the brief episode of the corner's bending, rather than a half-circle, prepares the horse's bending. What is shown now is easier than haunches-in on the center line. Here, moving along the wall, the pattern is easier, as the wall provides a guideline and security in preventing drifting of the horse away from the leg aids. Notice the precise angulation of the shoulder-in shown in this illustration, and by being along the wall, this angulation can also be monitored easier than along the center line.

Diagram: Barbara Leistico.

LATERAL BENDING ON TWO TRACKS 107

Elizabeth Ball on Bolshoj is riding a haunches-in to the left at the trot. Notice how the outside forehand of the horse must "merely" cross in front of the inside forehand's footprint. One also can see the exercise's secondary value for loosening the shoulders and adding to the strength and weight-bearing abilities of the inside legs. Photo: Richard F. Williams.

hibited and not encouraged by proposing a haunches-in on purpose!

Just because the horse is able and willing to perform the haunches-in at the canter, we should absolutely deny it. Later I will discuss how to correct a horse's evading with the haunches inward at the canter. I will explain why I do not recommend the haunches-in even as a preparation for canter pirouette work. In short, I recommend that haunches-in work be done mostly at the trot. At the walk, besides teaching values, it can be used to prepare certain movements or correct others.

The haunches-in should be performed so that it always leaves four tracks behind. Therefore it is not the "flip side" of the shoulder-in, a vastly different movement. Often riders fail to maintain a proper, continuous, inward torso flexion during the haunches-in. When the horse evades by counter-flexing and bending around the outside "displacing" leg of the rider, we then get a shoulder-out. For the definition of lateral movements

Susan Derr Drake is riding Will Power in a haunches-in to the right. I want to show close up how the rider's outside leg is very important. For it both creates the lumbar bending and the displacement of the haunches of the horse. The inside leg of the rider "hangs draped" vertically under the seat.

Photo: Paul Drake.

the bending of the horse's torso is just as important as the way his limbs travel and cross.

The haunches–out, the same movement as the haunches–in, is so named because of the change in the horse's relative position to the wall along which he travels. During haunches–in the horse's neck remains parallel to the wall of the manege on the outside track while the spine is bent inward placing the haunches on an inside track. The haunches must be bent inward enough to cross the legs well under and leave four distinct tracks in the sand. During haunches–out the horse's forehand is ridden on an inside track, away from the wall. This creates the room to ride the haunches out to the track at the wall. The horse's neck is still kept parallel to the wall but on an inside track. The haunches are displaced outward by bending the spine toward the outside wall of the manege.

THE HALF-PASS AND FULL PASS

The half-pass is tested in standard competition tests. The full pass is not tested, but it is a valuable training and schooling movement, as it accentuates the virtues of the half-pass to the ultimate. Skeletal flexibility, muscular suppleness and strengthening balance are all exercised to an extraordinary degree during a full pass. The full pass should not be ignored just because it has less drilling appeal to those who ride merely for success in competition. It still has greater gymnastic value than the half-pass. These movements can be done, and beneficially so, in all three natural gaits, the walk, trot and canter. The half-pass and full pass are the "kings" of two-track travel because extreme skill and precision are needed both by rider and horse to handle the exacting relationship required of the forehand and the haunches in traveling sideways and forward. The outstanding qualities of half-passes come from the absolute mastery of the control by the rider and the absolute understanding and willingness of the horse to place the forehand relative to the haunches at a precise relationship.

In general, during the half and full passes the horse travels "nearly" parallel to the wall of the manege. Only the shoulders must lead slightly ahead of the hips. If the hips lead ahead of the shoulders, the horse performs a compromised haunches-in (haunches-fore) on a diagonal line of travel. This is a serious evasion because the horse does not need to use his hip nor his shoulders as we want him to.

During the half- and full passes horses must remain bending in the direction toward which they travel. In fact, in all movements except the shoulder-in, this is a requirement. Therefore, the haunches-in, half-pass and pirouettes are strongly related by two uncompromisable standards:

1. They all are performed with the horse laterally bending toward the direction of his progress.
2. They all leave four tracks behind. The difference in lateral bending is substantial. At the haunches-in we require the most acute bending, as if on a volte (6m circle). At the half-pass a more modest amount of bending is acceptable as if

the horse were on an 8m to 10m circle, and the least amount of bending is possible during a pirouette (or partial) where the horse is mildly bent as if progressing on a 20m circle.

During a half or full pass, horses must straddle with the outside legs past the inside legs, both front and hind. "Crossing" means putting the outside or inside leg just in front of the other one, much as a tightrope walker would. But "straddling" means crossing the legs so acutely that the crossing leg will pass the other by some distance, the limbs forming an X when viewed from the front or from behind. During the half-pass the sideways progression is somewhat less than in the full pass, where we ask the horse to move as sharply sideways as possible without losing the essential perfection of bending, impulsion and cadenced suspension of the strides. The half-pass is easier, as it is milder in its demands on the horse's skills, strength and balance.

The half-pass has inimitable gymnastic value in freeing the elbows, loosening the shoulders, articulating the lumbar back and suppling the hips. Consequently, it is an eminent engagement exercise because it allows us to collect toward the haunches while lightening and liberating the forehand. The highly collected half-pass movement is one of the finest creators of the grand extensions.

THE COMPLETE OR PARTIAL PIROUETTE

Pirouettes represent the highest degree of collection at both the walk and the canter. The only way they can be imitated at the trot, however, is by slowly rotating a horse performing the piaffe! Therefore, if done at the trot, it is not a real pirouette, yet it is a movement certainly with unparalleled collection. We can agree that all pirouettes are best done when the horse's collection is maximized or impeccable. Uncollected pirouettes would be unacceptable and a contradiction in terminology.

The lowering of the haunches, the tucking with the lumbar back, the pushing of the hips forward and downward, the visual evidence of "sitting" are all essential to the pirouette. Performed at the canter, one must even school it with collection in mind.

Susan Derr Drake is riding Parmenio in a half-pass to the right in the frontal view and a half-pass to the left in the rear views. Notice that the horse's legs must straddle (cross) past the hoofprint left by the inside legs. Therefore, in half-pass a horse merely crossing in front of his inside hoofprints is not sufficiently engaged to make meaningful gymnastic progress. Half-passes should look like those shown in these pictures, where you can clearly see the outside legs straddling past the inside ones, forming an X.

In these pictures all is well: engaged limbs, evenly bent spine and torso, the shoulder slightly leading ahead of the hips in near parallel-to-wall position for progression. The deeper the legs can straddle without losing impulsion and bending, the more a horse approximates the full pass, which is not required in our competitions but essential for gymnastic suppling. The photograph opposite, above, comes close to a full pass, and displacement of the horse is more sideways than forward, emphasizing collection and engagement.

The half-pass offers the greatest challenge to the rider in showing total control over the relative positioning of the horse's haunches to the forehand. Riders must totally control the speed of progression of both ends of the horse to assure their unity and therefore the necessary bending and engagement. Photos: Paul Drake.

Arthur Kottas-Heldenberg, Chief Rider of the Spanish Riding School, is riding a full pass. Because of the moment at the trot, we can easily see the limbering of the horse's shoulders. And because of their great value in loosening the shoulders, the full pass and half-pass are indispensable to the development of a truly grand extended trot. Notice the beautiful bending, which is accomplished by impeccable equitation. Everything is in the right place, including the "silence" of the rider, which creates such tranquillity in the horse. Photo: Andreas Jarc.

Arthur Kottas-Heldenberg performing that rarely seen movement: a turn while performing the piaffe. This movement comes as close to a pirouette at the trot as possible. Yet the piaffe is more a passage in place than a trot, and therefore, we still do not consider the demonstrated movement a pirouette. Rather, it is a turning while at the piaffe.

One seldom can view such a fine piaffe. The lowering of the haunches causes the elegant byproduct of an elevated forehand, with a very tall rise to the horse's poll from the low crouch of his croup. By slowly rotating at the piaffe riders can school the horse's understanding of how to elevate his forehand and increase the articulation of the joints that allow the horse to "sit lower." As the horse sinks behind his rider, he rises in front of him. Yet the feet of the horse do not gather too close to make it impossible to leave the ground. Thus slow rotation at the piaffe can also be useful for the maximum "seating of the horse" without inducing too deep a gathering of the hind legs, which would result in a levade. Photo: Andreas Jarc.

Susan Derr Drake is riding Parmenio in a canter pirouette to the left. Notice particularly that the horse is in a true, three-beat canter. Supported only by the outside hind leg (the starting leg of the movement), he clearly elevates his other three limbs, thereby documenting to the observer that he is in a pure canter. Often, incorrectly ridden pirouettes corrupt the canter, and as the goal of all gymnastic work is the purity of the gaits, this picture shows that it can be maintained. Lowering the croup, bending evenly toward the direction of the turn, the horse executes his movement with balance, confidence and clarity of gait. Photo: Paul Drake.

Preceding any pirouette, turning around the inside hind leg, one should pursue a school canter, pure in gait, energetic in impulsion but so seated and slow that one thinks of bobbing in place. When this is done, one almost casually, and certainly very easily, can turn the horse around with one's outside leg and by rotating one's torso. Pirouettes, in spite of turning the horse around on a tiny spot, are not at all about turning. They are all about collection, lumbar flexibility and assumption of weight in the haunches. The horse, anchored much like a crane, lifts and turns the forehand with ease. Riders who mistake pirouettes for "turning jobs," and who do not understand it as collection, will not succeed.

Pirouettes and half-passes are never easy. But they are easier to perform at the walk than at the canter. Impulsion, suspension, momentum are so essential to these brilliant engagement exercises. At the walk you may want to teach the horse the "language" of your controls for these movements. However, once he understands what you want, practice half-passes and pirouettes mostly at the canter. Half-passes and full passes at the trot are valuable only if there is no loss of suspension. If cadence diminishes and the horse falls flatly to the ground and merely "scrapes sideways" as is very often the case, the half-pass loses its gymnastic value. In the canter we do not have to contend with that danger because it is a naturally bounding movement; the bending of the horse is ensured by the anatomy of the canter movement, which is always a laterally bent gait!

Susan Derr Drake is schooling Parmenio at a walk pirouette. Collection and obedience both increase as the joints in the haunches must increase their vertical articulation and collect to the maximum degree, while the shoulders (forehand) move with extended reaches to turn around the inside hind leg.

Photo: Paul Drake.

IMPROVING BENDING THROUGH LATERAL MOVEMENTS

The various patterns we ride are all gymnastic tools. When riding a circle, our aim is not just to return to the point of origin. Rather it is that the horse should remain perpetually and continuously bent along his spine. If he moves with consistent lateral bending, he will, incidentally, return to the point of origin. When discussing the gymnastic value of patterns, we must always keep in mind that more important than the spatial progression of the horse is the activity "within" his structure. Even when competing, the rider should not ride the test, rather he should ride his horse. Progression through space, passing over any tangle of patterns, becomes meaningless if the horse's skeletal and muscular development is not ensured by it.

For this reason we must distinguish between a horse performing a counter canter and one merely moving on the wrong lead. Just as we must discern the gymnastic difference between a horse traveling on a circle due to correct bending and one going back to his point of departure by way of a pentagon. Equally wrong would be to mistake any sideways drifting for a half-pass or shoulder-in, for instance.

Often the rider is not familiar with how a balanced horse, moving in good rhythm and cadence and correctly bent, feels. Perhaps the horse cannot yet oblige with bending aids because he is still too stiff. A two-track movement may not be performed well because the horse cannot discern the rider's aids.

Before reading the following about the quality of a shoulder-in, the reader should review the patterns shown in the illustration on page 119 because they will be discussed here.

One proceeds with the shoulder-in down the center line for a chosen number of steps, maybe all the way to X. This procession could be considered diagnostic. One may notice too much neck positioning as the horse evades bending throughout. Or one may detect a lack of impulsion or even coming above the bit due to the rider's overcontacting the inside rein. Whatever the shortcomings, the rider must diagnose them, speculate on their causes and determine the best ways to remedy them.

When arriving at X one asks for a walk and turns the horse

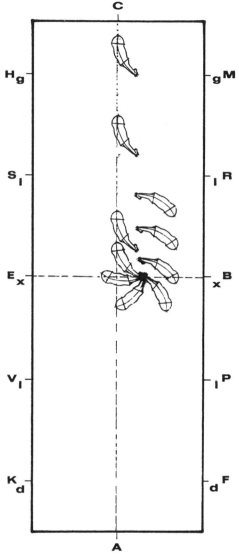

around his forehand with good impulsion and certainly without hesitation. The strong use of the inside leg and the softly yielding inside rein are necessary to this movement and will allow the horse to yield correctly, bending around the rider's inside leg and turning around his forehand 180 degrees. He will, by necessity, increase the crossing and lifting engagement of his inside hind leg and we can continue with a shoulder-in, returning to the short wall from where the movement started. One can elaborate on this movement by trotting after the pivoting around the forehand at X. Remember that the shoulder-in is most beneficial at the trot.

The shoulder-in after the pivot should be superior to the one that began this exercise and will likely have corrected many of the shortcomings noticed in the first shoulder-in. The reason for this is simple to understand because horse and rider will have learned, through the turn around the forehand, about the effectiveness of the rider's inside leg. A good shoulder-in largely depends on the correct use of the rider's inside leg. Placement, pressure, rhythm and the right muscular stimulus transferred to the horse's side are essential to success. The rider's outside leg, of course, as always when bending the horse, must be slightly farther back than the inside one, passively holding the haunches to maintain the needed curvature of the horse's spine behind the saddle.

All major faults in aiding a shoulder-in come from the horse's lack of obedience to the rider's inside leg. From that results frustration, and the rider multiplies his errors by pelvic gyrations, pulling the inside rein or kicking fast with drawn-up heels.

Should the rider opt to give the horse this lesson without any walk, he would have to replace the pivoting action at X with the following modification. Arriving at X, the rider can move on a half-circle from X to B with the horse's head in and tail out in a modified leg-yield. Then from B the rider continues to return to the short wall by a corrected shoulder-in.

The most effective introduction to a shoulder-in remains the riding of a circle preceding it. It is important to understand that the circle assists with the bending and that by starting a second circle ever so briefly to take the shoulders off the wall, pre-positions the horse for progression on two tracks. The horse ought to feel as if a second circle were proposed but, instead, he is ridden outward, away from the inside leg, along the wall. Perhaps plan a few, maybe only four steps of shoulder-in before repeating the circle. By repeating circles and progressing from one to the next with a few steps of shoulder-in, both horse and rider gain an understanding of the shoulder-in movement. The circle allows for frequent corrections of the rider's equitation and for correction of bending, impulsion and suspension in the horse. It is essential that the rider's inside leg remain both the leg prompting impulsion, as it always is, and the leg for displacing the horse. This double responsibility places expectations on the impeccable position and rhythmic effectiveness of the inside leg.

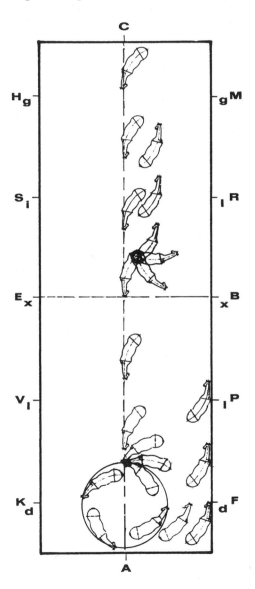

Equally important is the somewhat back-and-down-stretched position of the outside leg, which, with constant gentle adhesiveness, secures the horse's perpetual bending and prevents his "escaping" by throwing the haunches outward, off the track. The inside rein's contact must be supple and often willing to yield and never retroactive (pulling!). All of these equitational requirements can be monitored, checked, and corrected during the circles and leave a more perfect rider ready to ride a few good steps of shoulder-in for connecting the circles.

Bending can best be improved by the use of the rider's outside leg. Lateral bending occurs *around* the rider's inside leg but heavily depends on the careful use of his *outside* leg. The rider's outside leg actually does the bending. The horse finds bending the neck easy but bending his torso is much more difficult, especially around his lumbar area. The area behind the saddle remains the least flexible yet the most crucial for suppleness and certainly for the ability to collect.

Therefore, the haunches-in exercise is most appropriate for the creation of lateral bending. That is its major mission, and as mentioned earlier, it also strengthens the stifles and hips. Two sets of exercises can emphasize lumbar flexibility and good lateral bending. A horse ridden haunches-in along the center line can be half-pirouetted at the walk before resuming his progression toward the short wall with his haunches-in. If done at the trot, the pirouette episode will have to be done at the walk, and as this involves two transitions, the exercise becomes even further sophisticated in its value for collection.

If a trot is to be maintained throughout, the haunches-in can be followed by a circle with the haunches-in position maintained. And just to be sure the horse continues his work, as he should, between *both* legs of the rider, the circle is departed toward the corner by a brief episode of shoulder-in but immediately followed by haunches-in along the long wall. This exercise maintains the bending in the same direction but includes a short episode when the horse must cross and increase articulation with his inside hind leg during the shoulder-in.

Eleven

Sophisticated Gymnastic Patterns

There are a great many gymnastically useful patterns that can be ridden. Their numbers are infinite if we consider that combining gymnastic patterns with one another changes their functions in rehabilitation, restoration and athletic progress. Beyond the complications that come from combinations, we can further change the meaning and value of exercises by changing the gaits of the horse while riding them, and performing these patterns with transitions from gait to gait. Analogous to the Gestalt theory in psychology, with the patterns we ride we can claim that the *result is more than the sum of its parts*. For it is in the *configuration and combination* that the meaning resides. *Gestalt* means "configuration" in German, and reminds us that in riding the combinations of the pattern elements create the situation. Depending on the way we arrange and combine our patterns, the final results will be highly varied. All patterns must show scholarly relevance to one or more of these training goals: rehabilitation, restoration, correction, or athletic development. Patterns that lack "building" qualities and break the horse down, should be banished from use.

The scientific, scholastic nature of equitation cannot be

overemphasized. Riders must learn and know the gymnastic developmental goals for the horse, and they must know the best ways and means to attain them. Indeed, the means for the attainment of goals are often different from practicing the desired results. We do not get a horse straight by riding him on a straight street for miles. We do not point a horse from Boston to Philadelphia and plan to have him arrive there straight. We cannot school a three-year-old young and green and ungymnasticized horse in passage to get passage. We do many things, most of which are different exercises from those which we hope to attain eventually. Therefore, we must be aware that practicing seeming "opposites" of what we want often will help us attain our original intent. Straightness comes from lateral flexibility and frequent bending. Collection comes from working in the medium or extended versions of the gaits. Extensions benefit from collection, especially when executed at the shoulder-in or half-pass.

I will now concentrate on explaining a few of the many less-known and unfortunately seldom-used patterns that are particularly important gymnastic "tools" for developing horses. While this discussion will purposely omit the most commonly known and practiced patterns, I do, of course, recommend their use.

Controlling the horse's haunches is of utmost importance. In fact, the degree to which the rider can control the behavior and whereabouts of the horse's haunches, from which all energy for locomotion emanates, is the degree to which he can succeed in gymnastically developing his horse. For we *cannot shape our horse, only his energies!*

HAUNCHES-IN PATTERNS

The haunches-in is a difficult movement to teach a horse to perform correctly. However, it is a movement without which there can be no progress. There is no substitute for the developments that will take place as a result of using it. In the illustration on page 126 you will see a very basic pattern, which is most useful when performed at the walk. One teaches two-track

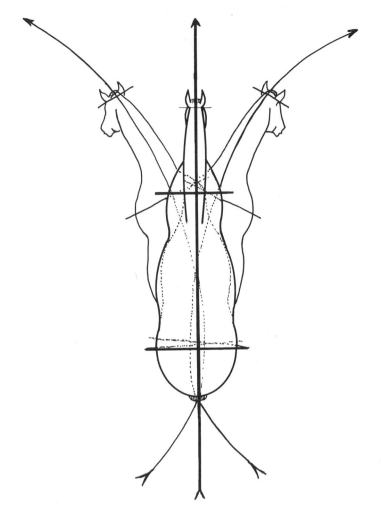

Horses can straighten only as a consequence of lateral flexibility achieved by bending. No horse can be kept straight merely by being kept straight on a path. Riders cannot through precision of influence alone make a horse strong and supple enough to move straight. Only by suppling, strengthening and elasticizing with laterally bent exercises can we then correct horses to move straight through our influence.

Horses should bend with equal facility right or left after the first year of training. Often, gravely mistaken, riders rock the horse's head side to side by pulling on the reins alternately. Or they twist the horse's neck from side to side and develop the illusion of a soft and supple horse followed by the delusion of a well-bent horse. Only correctly, evenly bent horses will athletically improve.

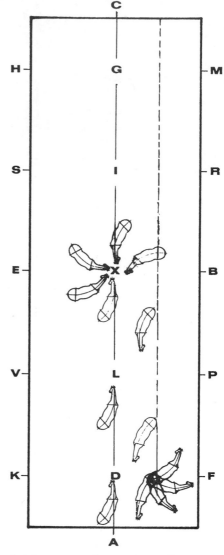

movements to the horse and rider most often at the walk. However, the haunches-in should be performed at the trot as soon as it has been taught and well schooled since many of its benefits (among them the strengthening of the stifles and lumbar back) come when it is done at the trot rather than at the walk.

Starting down the center line (shown here with a left bend), one performs the haunches-in followed by a counter change of hand, which is here a pivoting around the forehand, and then return toward the short wall with the haunches-out. After a few steps of haunches-out, one can perform a half-pirouette (turning around the haunches) and continue along the wall either straight or with another haunches-in.

As with all patterns, this one can be elaborated on in many ways. For example, the counter change around the forehand at X can be continued until the horse returns to the center line (because of the 360-degree pivot), on which he could continue to C with his haunches-in. Or, for instance, one could continue from the pirouette (near F) with a half-pass to V. From there one could continue with a haunches-out along the wall for a while before straightening.

Regardless of how elaborate or how simple the combinations of patterns, we always should emphasize to the horse the importance of bending, the finest engagement on the crossing outside hind leg and the best possible weight-bearing on the inside hind leg. Many horses with a weak left hind begin to gimp in a "rein-lame" fashion and become both unlevel and arhythmic. In extreme cases, they appear as if ready to collapse over the left hind leg, especially when it is the inside hind leg.

The basic pattern shown in the illustration on page 128 is also based on the value of the haunches-in. One starts with the haunches-in down the center line and then one performs a half-pirouette, which one finishes in a shoulder-in position to continue in the shoulder-in movement. By doing partial pirouettes, one can continue to alternate between episodes of haunches-in and shoulder-in. The value is great in maintaining the same bending (here to the left) but the hind leg that must cross under changes with the change from haunches-in to shoulder-in. In the haunches-in the outside hind leg is crossing and the weight-bearing shifts to the inside hind leg. Here both stifles are worked. The collection relies on the articulation at the lower back (lumbar), the hip and stifle. During the shoulder-in, however, the inside hock is being strengthened primarily, thereby articulating and enhancing collection. Because the crossing inside hind leg must also move well forward during shoulder-in and because it must cross from the hollow inside toward the stretched outside, it maintains the weight-bearing functions as well.

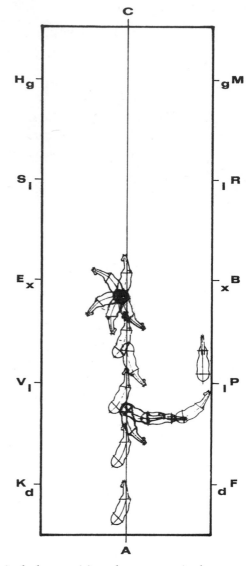

Elaborations can include transitions between gaits because pirouettes and pivots must be done at the walk and not at the trot. Ample opportunities for transitions are important for enhancing the collection value of these exercises. One can also add, both from haunches-in or shoulder-in, a half-pass. The meaning, function and "worth" of the half-pass vary greatly, depending on whether it is started from a haunches-in (in which case the controlling of the horse's shoulder "pirouetting forward" one-eighth of a turn is involved) or started from a shoulder-in (where the shoulders already slightly lead as they ought to for the half-pass). The difficulty is in "gathering" the haunches for engagement without losing the lumbar bending. Whenever one runs out of space in the manege, one can use a pivot around the forehand to facilitate a change of direction and continue the same exercise proceeding in the opposite direction.

One must always mirror exercises by riding them on both hands, alternately. After all, the goal is to create an "ambidextrous athlete" from a "one-handed," naturally crooked horse.

The pattern shown on page 130 is of great usefulness because horses respond and grow with it. One walks with the haunches-in and terminates it by beginning a pivot around the forehand. This causes an increased displacement of the haunches, which in turn softens the bending and strengthens collection of the outside hind leg. After a half pivot of 180 degrees around the forehand, one changes by new controls over the horse's forehand and shoulder to a pirouette.

In this exercise the bending (in the illustration bending is to the right) of the horse remains constant, but there is a crucial moment when from the pivot around the forehand we change to a pirouette around the inside hind leg. The outside hind leg of the horse always remains engaged! The bending is always the same. Yet the change from great control of the haunches to great control over the shoulders (forehand) makes a dramatic difference for the horse. The resolution of this exquisite "control exercise" can be either a haunches-in, a half-pass or at the least, because of shifting to the inside leg for crossing, a shoulder-in.

The illustration on page 130 is strongly related to the preceding exercises. Here, too, we intensify the control over the horse's haunches, increase the engagement of the outside hind leg (mostly at the hip and stifle) and insist on maintaining, and improving, the bending to the same side (here to the left). We repeatedly ride the horse from haunches-in to half-pass and haunches-in again. With such patterning we must review the increasing and decreasing of lateral bend (more at haunches-in and less at half-pass) while we consolidate our control over the flexibility of the spine and torso due to proper engagement of the haunches.

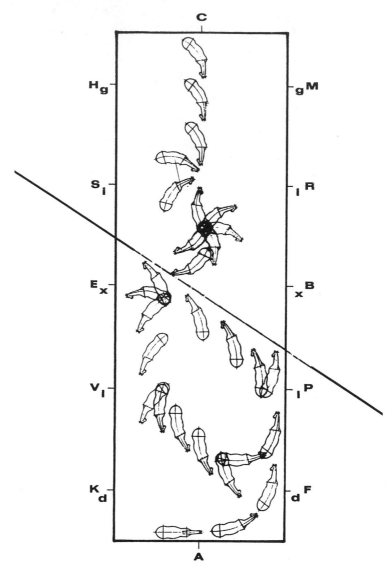

COUNTER PATTERNS

The next group of patterns discussed and illustrated can most appropriately be performed at the trot. However, they can be used at the walk although with less gymnastic value and, with appropriate modifications, inspire work at the canter.

The illustration on page 131 shows the fundamental pattern of a counter change of hand. In a true change of hand the rider

THE ATHLETIC DEVELOPMENT OF THE DRESSAGE HORSE

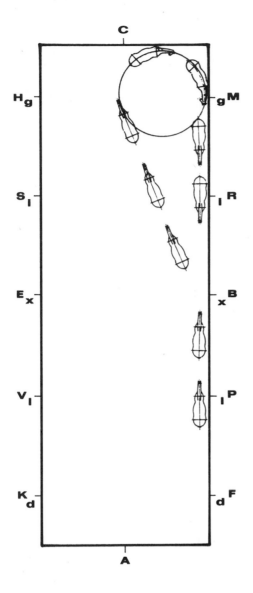

would proceed from the wall, through a half-circle and then, on a straight line, return diagonally to the wall, facing the opposite direction from which he started. During the counter change, however, the rider starts by proceeding diagonally away from the wall and returns to it by way of a half-circle outward, toward the wall.

Counter changes are enormously important even though they are all too infrequently used. With counter patterns riders can learn the exactitude in the dimensions of patterns. Dimensions cannot be larger because there is a wall containing them and they need not fall short because the wall guides the rider exactly to where he ought to be. For instance, to ride an exact 10m circle, the counter pattern will guarantee its size. Riding a circle inward, as a true pattern, can easily result in a larger or smaller circle than desired.

Ultimately, the rider can work on a walk or canter pirouette outward (counter pattern) toward the wall to ensure that the horse does not move forward to evade but remains on the spot, since the presence of the wall compels him to do so. Regarding the pirouette toward a wall, the rider must remember that the horse can use many other evasions. To avoid having him substitute new evasions for the relatively mild one of making too large a circle with the hind legs during a pirouette, the rider should only practice such pirouette exercises on well-schooled, collected and mature horses. This should not be a teaching but rather a polishing exercise.

The basic pattern we see in this illustration can lend itself to many useful elaborations. I will describe a few of them.

VARIATIONS

- Make the diagonal departure from the wall steeper, approximating arrival at the quarter line rather than at the center line. This produces a tighter half-circle, which is really a half-volte now, before reversing direction. One must feel the horse's limits in bending and collection and note any diminishing of impulsion or cadence as grave signs that the horse is being overtaxed.
- Or one can depart at a canter, at the mid-point of the half-circle, where it touches the short side of the arena. If performed correctly, this exercise is wonderful for producing well-engaged canter departures and for helping horses depart on a lead they are usually reluctant to use. Note that if the canter does not depart during the period of bending, the exercise loses its value.

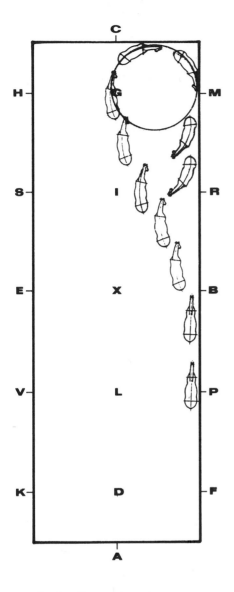

- In the illustration above you can see an elaboration by using two-track movements. One may leave the wall with a leg-yield, and maintain the engagement of the crossing hind leg so as to continue with a shoulder-in along the wall.
- When the engagement is good enough, one may continue, after the half-circle, along the wall by extending the strides from M to F. This usually produces exceptionally good re-

sults due to the intelligent preparation. One might elaborate also by doing a shoulder-in from M to B and from there cross the arena to K in an extension or lengthening of strides.

Looking at the illustration below, one can see how these changes can be used for preparation of the half-passes, here shown from B to K. When a half-pass is asked for out of a

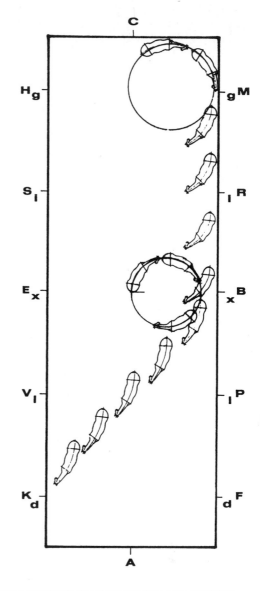

shoulder-in, the rider must change the emphasis of control from the engagement of the inside hind leg to the engagement of the outside leg. This is so difficult for both horse and rider that it is often necessary to insert a circle, to regain impulsion and carriage, and continue with the half-pass after having afforded the preparation through the circle.

During all of these difficult patterns, one must be perpetually alert to maintain good impulsion. The rhythmic regularity must remain impeccable and uncompromised. Slowing or hurrying during such exercises are serious signs of either disobedience or warnings of inability to execute them because of unpreparedness. The horse is our calendar. We must never overdemand and stress him physically beyond his means of readiness. We should never cause him to mistrust us because we ask for undue performance. The horse alerts his rider when he is not ready gymnastically to perform a movement. He signals precisely by changing rhythm, level of impulsion and degree of cadencing elevation.

I advise strongly against riding haunches-in at the canter. In fact, one of the most serious and yet common disobediences at canter includes the "throwing of haunches inward" by the horse. Because the canter is always a movement in which the horse by necessity is bent toward his lead, we must be keenly aware of the ease with which he can avoid engagement by curving with his haunches inward. This version of the crooked horse will disengage and especially prevent the proper action with his inside hind leg. Later, I will spend considerable energies in this book discussing how to improve the canter. Suffice to say here that the canter should be ridden straight with the horse's inside shoulder traveling directly in front of his inside hip.

Another warning to be mentioned here: doing too much lateral work at the walk can cause the deterioration of that important gait. Therefore the rider must often lengthen the reins and allow the horse to stretch his neck forward and downward to a free walk. The accordion effect of the topline's stretching and contracting becomes most important when teaching lateral exercises. Whether on contact and in collection, or stretched freely on a loose rein, the horse should walk with good impulsion. Never allow a lazy stroll, but keep a marching attitude.

During the counter-change exercises in the trot, the rider may often increase the horse's tempo by driving for a stronger, longer, trot. During the "critical periods" in these exercises, the rider should urge onward quite strongly. An aware rider is particularly alert to any slackening of energy, any sense of the horse striding more flatly or more choppily than before. In such a case, one should immediately drive the movement to its possible crescendo and confirm to the horse an increased tempo.

Twelve

Suppling Patterns at the Trot

Suppling at the trot is particularly useful because in this gait suspension and rhythm are most easily monitored and influenced.

Ride shoulder-in on the short walls, after having made sure of well-bent yet single-track corners preceding them. Also, after the shoulder-in, remember to straighten the horse for the long wall. Since one of the important training principles is that we ought to follow collection with extension, a rider could lengthen strides on the long walls and promote collection only during the short walls where the shoulder-in is performed.

- Greatly challenging, with high gymnastic value, is the riding of shoulder-in through the four corners of the school. This remains one of the finest challenges to the rider's equitational skills. Corners, being small arcs negotiated by deeply bent horses, become an exceptional challenge when performed on two tracks such as in a shoulder-in. Riding small arcs certainly can increase collection and can even promote the lumbar tucking and lowering of the horse's croup.
- Ride a 20m circle to start with, and then continue to spiral

in and out. The simplest way to do this is on a single track by very gradually decreasing and increasing the size of the circle. However, the most sophisticated version of this exercise remains when the diminishing of the circle is done by riding a half-pass to a 10m circle and expanding it with a shoulder-in, drifting outward to the original 20m circle.

Spirals are very sophisticated and necessary gymnastic exercises. They are suitable for a beginning horse and must be reviewed with increased sophistication with the advanced horse. We all know that the most sophisticated pattern of the canter, the pirouette, is often schooled through a spiral beginning. It is a pattern that is useful throughout the entire schooling life of the horse.

As much as the horse is gymnasticized by spirals, the rider benefits even more. A pattern that is enormously difficult to ride provides an excellent test of the rider's controls. It is hard enough to progress gradually inward from a 20m to a 10m circle, but to do it with total control over the shoulders and haunches is a truly great challenge. The more gradual the tightening of the spiral, the more sophisticated are the rider's controls. Just "slamming in" sideways is wrong, of course. On advanced horses, the final circle could be reduced to a volte, a circle with the diameter equal to twice the particular horse's length. Therefore, it is usually 6m. However, a new FEI decision designates "a volte as a circle from 5m to 8m in diameter."

Variations on the spiral theme are numerous. The illustration on the facing page, left side, shows the simplest of all. By progressing inward more gradually (like the needle on the grooves of a phonograph record) and going outward rather suddenly with a leg-yield, one can elaborate this deceptively simple exercise into a much more difficult one. Seldom are spirals controlled enough to be well placed symmetrically on either side of the center line. Usually we see an excuse for a major drift toward an oval or shapeless indentation, offset toward one wall as the horse moves "upstream" toward the drift of his outside shoulder on an irregular pattern.

The illustration on the facing page, right side, shows a spiral with a haunches-in at C and with a shoulder-in at A. One can further vary the task and make it much more sophis-

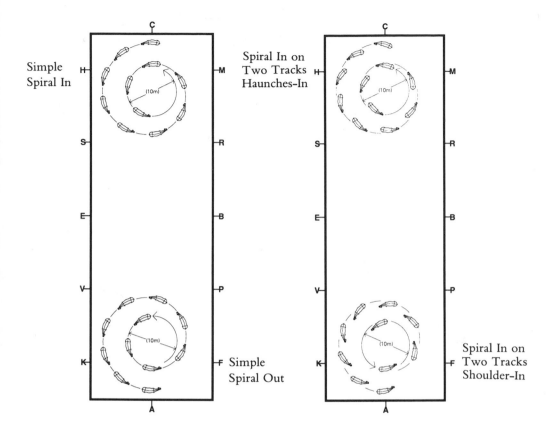

Simple Spiral In

Spiral In on Two Tracks Haunches-In

Simple Spiral Out

Spiral In on Two Tracks Shoulder-In

These two illustrations demonstrate what I discuss in detail below: the simplest variation (on the left) can be elaborated on to become much more difficult and the variation shown on the right can be made much more sophisticated by going inward with the haunches-in and going outward with the shoulder-in. Diagrams: Barbara Leistico.

ticated by intermingling these two propositions for spiraling with a horse on two tracks. Thus, one can diminish the circle with the haunches-in and enlarge the circle with the shoulder-in. This is the most logical way to make a spiral sophisticated. It is also a supreme test for the rider to control his horse with both of his legs, assuming that each is in its respective correct position: inside leg "on the girth," outside leg somewhat behind that.

Less logical but sometimes useful for specific schooling difficulties is to spiral inward with the shoulder-in and outward with the haunches-in. This outward movement could unwisely push the horse toward his outside shoulder. This is a common evasion that would promote this mistake, but in special cases, for reasons of lumbar suppling, we might want to use this exercise.

When riding such patterns as those above, one must remember the concepts and principles that make them useful. When first teaching a shoulder-in a rider must emphasize leg-crossing, and often the wisest decision is to slightly over-angle the movement and allow the horse to deliver it on four tracks. Later, with increased collection and increased torso bending, the horse will, voluntarily, deliver good shoulder-in correctly on three tracks.

From the rider's point of view the lightness and yielding of the inside rein is indispensable. The pulling, confining inside rein that exaggerates neck bending in the horse and arrests forward reaching of the inside hind leg is the equitational enemy of the shoulder-in. While the inside rein must remain supple and even yielding forward when necessary, the outside rein must not insist on contact so strong as to force a tilting of the muzzle of the horse outward and with it a lowering of the horse's inside ear. To allow or even teach a horse a severe evasion to bending, such as pivoting at the poll sideways with the head, has enormously negative consequences and, once learned by the horse, this is a grave mistake that is hard to correct.

As in all instances when the horse is laterally bent, especially during a shoulder-in, the rider's outside leg must be placed slightly behind the vertically hanging inside leg, around which the horse is invited to bend. The outside leg remains mostly passive and steadily, constantly and consistently wrapped onto the horse. It should feel as if one is receiving the horse's swinging ribcage. But by being correctly placed, back from the hip and thigh and yet with deep heel and well-flexed ankle, the outside leg determines for the rider the correct placement of his center of gravity onto the inside seatbone. One is never "heavier" on one of the seatbones by artifice, such as grinding downward pressure, or worse yet, leaning toward it like a motorcycle rider. One simply, naturally, without effort, sits always on the "inside seatbone," the one on the "hollow side" of the horse, when one's outside leg is placed behind the vertically hanging inside one.

While discussing the shoulder-in, perhaps this is the most appropriate place to remind riders that all controlling of the horse's neck must be at the base of the neck, that is, at the withers. The withers and shoulders must be the focus of our efforts in controlling the horse's forehand. A grave mistake is to separate the hands and steer the horse's muzzle hither and yon, twisting his neck often into painful overbending. It is never the where-abouts of the muzzle that we need to control. If a rider has mastered the control and the location of his horse's shoulder by controlling the base of the neck at the withers, the rest of the neck and at the end of it the properly, loosely hanging head of the horse will find its right location. Of course, a horse's neck and head are inward away from the wall during a shoulder-in but never because they are pulled in, merely because they extend beyond the shoulders and withers which happen to be about 33 degrees inward from the wall. As neck and head continue from the withers, they will be in the right place and correctly relaxing only if the shoulders and withers are placed correctly.

THE IMPORTANCE OF TWO-TRACK EXERCISES

"Two-track" is a generic expression referring to all the exercises during which the horse's shoulders travel on a path different from but parallel to that of his haunches. However, during "two-track" exercises the horse will leave three or four different tracks on the ground with his hoofprints.

The shoulder-in is the alpha and omega of "two-track" exercises. For in a way, it is the simplest of them all and so it is introduced earliest in the horse's training on "two tracks." It is in other ways, however, the most sophisticated of all "two-track" movements simply because it is the only one in which we ask the horse to move in the direction opposite the bending of his torso. A horse performing the shoulder-in left will be bent left but will travel and progress toward the right. The rider feels as though the movement is progressing from his left leg (both impulsion and displacing the horse at the same time) toward his right elbow, at which the rider "receives and modifies" the exercise. Again, remember the general principle of good equitation that everything is done with legs and seat; the role of the hands is to modify the excesses of the other two. Hands are moderators, negotiators but not creators of movements. Nor should hands ever define the patterns by steering. All that must be done with legs and seat!

Except for the shoulder-in, all other two-track movements belong to the same general category. They are all performed with the horse progressing toward the direction toward which he is bent. They are all based on the outside legs crossing in front of the inside legs. This, of course, creates the all-important skills for the horse to tuck the pelvis forward, lower the croup and round the lumbar back. The flexibility of the haunches that results in the "vertical accordion" that seats the horse more on the haunches all comes from these two-track exercises: the haunches-in, the half-pass, the full pass (not shown in competition) and the full and partial pirouettes. There are slight, yet gymnastically important and meaningful differences among these interrelated two-track exercises.

The haunches-in is the most difficult "two track" exercise to perform correctly for both horse and rider, and it has great strengthening, therefore suppling, value for the stifle joints. These are "open" and weak joints that often are responsible for unlevel strides in the hind legs, also the horse's inability to suspend and an easily visible forward dragging of the toes of the hind feet during the trot. These dragging toes are often even "bumping along" the uneven ground that has lumps of dirt in the footing. Even with the most genetically athletic horses, there is much work to be done for the proper strengthening of the stifles, and it can best be done with the help of haunches-in exercises. The horse ought to bend continuously with suppleness in the direction of his progress and perform the movements on four tracks (unlike the shoulder-in). While the outside hind leg crosses under, it is being elasticized, and the inside hind leg must carry the brunt of the weight, which lands on it with great impaction. At the beginning of haunches-in work, most horses show unlevel strides, loss of impulsion, flattening strides with loss of suspension and a loss of the purity in the trot gait. Gradually things ought to improve. As they do, all other movements and exercises will improve noticeably, as the side effects of the therapeutic and strengthening value of this most demanding exercise are realized. Of the three interrelated exercises we discuss here, the haunches-in demands the greatest lateral bending.

The half-pass should be ridden with medium intensity of lateral bending; less than during haunches-in but more than during the pirouette. The legs must "straddle" past the hoofprints of the inside, leading legs. The lumbar back and the hip joints gain the greatest benefit from this exercise. The outside hip must lower and tuck as the outside hind leg straddles in front of and past the hoofprint of the inside one. Here too the inside hind leg, especially at the hip joint, will become the weight-bearing one that carries most of the impaction. The horse must not "deflate" but indeed should show great ability to remain in "dancing suspension" when performing half-passes at the trot. Also in the canter, the "bounding" suspension must be retained.

Pirouette demands a great deal of collection but slightly less lateral bending than the half-pass. Like the shoulder-in, the pirouettes are taxing on the hocks. The hocks must work with great vertical articulation, and as a consequence the weight should shift so much toward the haunches that the croup visibly lowers, especially in the canter pirouette.

COMBINING TWO-TRACK EXERCISES

Combining various two-track exercises can increase their rehabilitative, therapeutic and gymnastic values enormously. These ambitious exercises also increase and refine the rider's skills, and thus benefit the rider's equitation to a degree unparalleled in other riding practices.

When combined, two-track exercises can be organized into four basic categories:

1. Those where the bending of the horse remains the same and the order of leg crossing of the horse also remains the same.
2. Those where the bending of the horse remains the same but the leg crossing order changes.

3. Those where the bending of the horse changes but the leg crossing remains the same.
4. Those where both the bending of the horse and the order of leg crossing change.

Examples of these types of combinations would include the following:

1. A horse can trot in shoulder-in from K to E and then half-pass from E to G without changing his bending to the right. However, he will need to cross first with his inside legs and after that with his outside legs. The rider's skills must include the ability to maintain a continuous lateral bend in the horse while changing leg influences. And he must sustain impulsion and rhythm with his inside leg throughout the exercise. Not a small task, and it requires polished skills.
2. A very important combination exercise is to start again from K, for example, with a half-pass right for four steps followed by a shoulder-in parallel with the long wall for four steps. This to be followed once again with a half-pass and finishing with a shoulder-in and turning, right of course, as the whole example of this sequence was for a horse in right lateral bending. This exercise is most effective in preventing a horse in half-pass from losing his balance by rushing toward the leading shoulder, or from losing his bending by leaning and bulging onto the inside shoulder, eventually assuming a counter flexion. Intermingling half-pass with shoulder-in remains one of the most important bending, suppling and balancing exercises for the all-around development of the horse.
3. An example of combinations when only the bending changes but the crossing of legs continues is to change from a shoulder-out to a haunches-in.
4. An example of combinations when both the bending and the crossing of legs change would be as follows: Start down the center line and ride a shoulder-in left from A to X. Then from X to C ride a shoulder-out (which equals the shoulder-in to the right).
5. One can combine exercises in which both bending and the

crossing with the outside legs over the inside ones is maintained. These would simply be continuous combinations of the three interrelated two-track movements, that of the haunches-in, the half-pass and the pirouette. One can follow this pattern as an example: from K to E along the wall, ride a haunches-in. Follow it from E to G by a half-pass and at G perform (at the walk or canter) a half-pirouette. This can be followed by a choice of either half-pass right back to the wall of origin or by doing less than half a pirouette, continue on the center line toward A with a haunches-in. This in turn can continue infinitely by doing another half-pass or half-pirouette, which once again can revert to a haunches-in, and so on.

I call these combined two-track exercises done in a continuous fashion, "ribbon exercises." They are most useful in the trot when impulsion and suspension can best monitor the level of engagement. However, all two-track exercises can best be taught at the walk. At this gait both horse and rider can better understand the skills these very complex exercises are based on. Some of these exercises, notably the pirouette, cannot be performed at the trot, only at the walk or canter. Therefore, one ought to practice some good "ribbon exercises" at the walk, such as the ones I suggest below:

- Walk from K to V with haunches-in. Proceed from V to X at the half-pass. Continue from X to G in another haunches-in. Half pirouette at G, and half-pass from G to E.

Elaborate if you wish by continuing with more two-track exercises that may include more of the above exercises, or add shoulder-in and even full pirouette. When finished the exercises at the walk, trot or canter work is advisable as a reminder that all good riding is forward with energy! Another "ribbon exercise" is as follows:

- At the walk half-pass right from K to the center line. On the center line turn counterclockwise around the forehand. Then half-pass right from the center line back to K.

A turn on the forehand (or pivot), of course, is not a good engagement exercise, and I consider it a bit "counter dressage" because it encourages the horse to lean to and dwell on the forehand. Yet I recommend it because it has enormous value in sensitizing the horse to the message of the rider's outside leg, especially as relevant for the displacement of the horse's haunches. One of the most important communication devices in the "alphabet" of equitation is to teach the horse that you wish to control the haunches sideways, "unilaterally," and have him obey that message. When taught through the pivot, the horse quickly understands that this leg pressure does not urge forward, onward and speed: precisely because of the requirement to dwell on the forehand, the horse cannot "escape forward" and will learn to turn away from pressure. This, as discussed much earlier, is really contrary to the horse's genetically coded claustrophobic instincts. These instincts suggest that the horse move "into the rider's pressuring leg" and oppose it. Thus, there is great value in any exercise that teaches the horse the "cultured" reaction of moving away from leg pressure rather than toward it as instinct would dictate!

The value of two-track exercises can be further increased if one can enhance them by incorporating some transitional work. This keeps the horse alert and keenly impulsive as well as mindful of the engagement of his quarters. All transitions demand some engagement because the center of gravity and the horse's balance must necessarily change. An example of incorporating transitions to enhance the value of "ribbon-exercises" follows:

- In the walk half-pass right from K to the center line. Half-pirouette on the center line. Then immediately depart in right lead canter and canter straight up the center line to turn right at A.

  Pattern suggestions emphasizing the shoulder-in could include the following exercise, which can be done at the trot or walk but preferably at the trot:

- Turn on the center line and from A to X do shoulder-in to the left. At X 10m circle first left, then right (a figure-8) and continue from X to C down the center line with shoulder-in to the right.

Remember that these circles are wonderful for correcting any problems that may have emerged during the shoulder-in, as they improve impulsion, suspension and balance toward the haunches. Equally important is the chance to reconfirm that the lateral bending of the horse is even and continuous!

- Ride a shoulder-in left from F to B and then turn left to ride from B to E on the half-arena line. Turn right at E and conclude by riding a shoulder-in right from E to H.

The short episode of straight riding on the half-arena line can be a wonderful instrument for increasing impulsion by either a medium trot or on advanced horses by riding passage. More intriguing ideas can include a canter left after the turn at B, with a flying change at X and reverting to the trot just before turning right at E. The possibilities of these combinations are endless. After all, one can change direction, bending, gaits and length of both stride and posture until only imagination and the horse's gymnastic development set the limits on what wonderful patterns can and may be done.

FURTHER THOUGHTS ABOUT THE TWO-TRACK MOVEMENTS

Some of the best engagement exercises are done on two tracks. To be sure, changing speed by extending and collecting strides within a gait without changing tempo is another excellent way to engage a horse. But insofar as engagement depends greatly on the horse's attentiveness to the rider, lateral exercises, which demand more submission by the horse to the aids, often do the job of engagement most effectively.

Engagement presupposes the mental condition of attentiveness. That is followed by acceptance of the rider's influences, resulting in obedience to the rider's aids and maturing into submission based on trust.

The above-described mental state leads to physical conditions of engagement that will be manifested by the horse doing better than ever before due to increased attention. Habitual use of the haunches with vigor and increased flexion in the joints are additional signs of engagement. So are any signs of collection (i.e., shifting the center of gravity toward the haunches) as are transitions showing clarity and active support from the haunches.

Achievement of the above results in advanced engagement is evidenced by the lowering of the croup. Concurrently there is increased bending of the hind leg joints, both when the limbs leave the ground and also, more importantly, when the limbs impact on the ground and support the weight. This produces the elevation of the forehand at the withers and the raising of the entire torso while in motion. Engaged horses always feel "taller" to their riders and as if they are "traveling uphill." All these signs of engagement are crowned by the consistent maximization of delivery of all the essentials of each of the gymnastic exercises. The "definitive components" of exercises are maximized, such as the straddling of the legs during a half-pass or the lowering of the croup during piaffe or pirouette.

THE NATURE OF TWO-TRACK MOVEMENTS

The two-track gymnastic exercises that engage the horse most effectively, both mentally and physically, can most easily be performed at the walk. After having practiced them at the walk, and having attained engagement manifest in exact rhythm, active haunches and exact patterning, one can continue with these exercises at the trot. Often at the trot the patterns must be slightly altered. All short turns, pirouettes, etc., will need to be enlarged to full or partial circles. All good riders understand how to enlarge pivots and pirouettes at the walk to their larger equivalents at the trot.

There exist many possibilities for the elaboration of combinations of two-track exercises, particularly if one uses counterchanging patterns for short about-turns. These exercises are especially useful for the physical flexing of the horse as well as increasing his mental attentiveness.

Some caution is in order, however. After practicing "ribbon exercises" in the walk, which is necessarily collected and on contact, one ought to return to a free walk on a long rein to rest. It is important to regain the walk, a gait that is often ruined by being ridden too much or exclusively on contact. Also, relaxation and stretching after difficult exercises remains both physically and mentally important for the horse.

Explosive, impatient young horses would not benefit much from these movements, which demand training sophistication from both horse and rider. Premature drilling of these exercises can be harmful and can also cause resistance. However, indefinitely delaying more difficult tasks can also be counterproductive in training strategies. Progress can only be made by challenging the status quo.

Any time a horse shows frustration or confusion, examine yourself to be sure your aids are clear, harmonious, light and done while retaining perfect balance. Shifting balance by tilting, tensing, or gripping can be uncomfortable, even painful, rather than informative to the horse. Remember that communication succeeds not by exerting force and strength, but rather by timely, rhythmic delivery of light aids.

Care must be taken that rhythm is preserved and remains metronomically precise. Also, in two-track movements consistent angulation relative to the walls of the manege must be maintained. The bending of the spine of the horse must remain even and continuous. Abandoning or compromising the standards relative to angles, bending, rhythm, impulsion and purity of the gait seriously damages or annuls the merits of these efforts.

LATERAL BENDING ON TWO TRACKS: PRIMARY USES

The leg-yield introduces the horse to the acceptance of the rider's special leg aids that produce displacement of the horse sideways. Sideways motion rather than forward zest is a highly specific reaction to the rider's application of his leg influences. The leg-yield is most often the horse's first experience with sideways motion, and when perfected, should be performed with a rather straight torso and spine. Too much bending around the leg of pressure will cause an undesirable leaning toward the leading shoulder and a torso "broken at the withers" for exaggerated neck bending opposite the direction of motion. All of these are clumsy attempts by the horse to cope with the new way of balancing. The rider must help and guide the horse to move with as straight a torso as possible. Leg-yielding can be performed at the walk and at the trot. When it is approximated at the canter, it is called a "plié." The difference between plié and leg-yield is important: At the canter (plié) the horse should not cross or straddle his legs. The movement should produce the first acquaintance with collection, especially by increased articulation with the inside hock. It is also a body strengthening and rebalancing exercise at the canter.

With the shoulder-in and shoulder-out one can particularly activate and strengthen (therefore, supple) the inside hind leg of the horse and especially the hock joint. Almost as important, these exercises liberate and loosen the shoulders and further the skills of elevating the forehand. These movements have very high value in collecting and engaging the haunches and promoting increased muscular elasticity. With maximum lateral bending required of the horse's torso, we know that the horse must elastically expand his musculature on the outer side, while contracting it on the inner side of his torso. Both shoulder-in and shoulder-out can be performed at the walk or the trot. When an analogous movement is done at the canter, we call it a "shoulder-fore." Again, the monumentally important difference is in not allowing the horse to cross his legs while in canter. Instead, one moves his inside shoulder "to the fore," placing it directly in front of the inside hip. This brings the withers slightly inward from the wall and the horse's angulation from the wall remains much milder than the 33 degrees required for the shoulder-in.

The shoulder-fore is the paramount exercise for straightening at the canter. An almost unceasing task, considering that the canter is, by nature, a movement with lateral bend even if one wants to proceed along a straight line. Horses soon find the efficient evasion of engagement by moving their haunches slightly inward. As the hips are much wider than the shoulders, horses find that by "hugging" the wall with their head, neck, and shoulder, they can coil inward with their haunches, giving a despicable holiday to the inside hind leg, which ought to carry the brunt of the weight. By riding canter in a shoulder-fore, the problem can be solved, with the horse functionally straightened, but not geometrically straightened, he can be ridden into good engagement.

The haunches-in and the haunches-out are the best exercises for taking possession of the controlling of the haunches. This is crucial for straightening horses and encouraging the even loading and reaching of the hind legs. Lumbar flexibility and both lateral and vertical articulation of the lumbar back depend on these exercises. The strengthening of the stifle and to a lesser degree the hip joints also depend on these movements. In many ways these exercises are the kernel of the horse's athletic progress. It is very difficult to perform them properly and without severe loss of impulsion and elevation of strides to proper suspension. Therefore, often, when poorly done at the trot, the trot gait loses its purity. As we do not aim to destroy but rather perfect the natural gaits, we must remain cautious by doing these tasks gradually and on well-prepared horses.

Haunches-in and haunches-out can be done at all three gaits. However, I cannot caution riders enough to avoid permitting their horses to do haunches-in at the canter. This movement is the very choice of horses who try to avoid proper engagement. We lavish attention and effort on engaging the horse's inside hind leg during the canter. When asked or allowed to do haunches-in at the canter, the horse inevitably evades by throwing his haunches in and stiffening his inside hock. Haunches-in is often recommended as preparatory to pirouetteing at the canter. It is argued that haunches-in would produce the all-important lumbar bending and predispose the horse to a good pirouette. I disagree with this view. Exactly for the same reasons that leading with the haunches-in before a half-pass destroys the half-pass; leading with the haunches on approaching or even during pirouette work destroys the pirouette. The horse disengages his inside hind leg, permits himself to remain unseated and precludes the lowering of the croup and the submission of the topline through proper use of his inside hock. Far from being preparatory to pirouettes, the haunches-in at the canter can prevent pirouettes from ever properly developing.

The half-pass and the full pass (less forward, more sideways and with greater straddling of the legs) emphasize the ultimate art of the rider's lateral control of his horse. Unless the whereabouts of the horse's shoulder and haunches are precisely under the rider's control, the horse will never perform a brilliant half-pass. The half-pass is the "king" of lateral movement, proof of the precision of the relative position of forehand to haunches and thus proof that the rider is in command of his skills of straightening his horse! In a half-pass the rider must place the shoulder ever so slightly ahead of the haunches in progression, yet he must not lose the "functional" paralleling of the walls of the manege. The primary strengthening function of the half-pass addresses the hips, the all-important joint for the tucking of the pelvis, lowering of the croup and articulation of the lumbar region. The half- and full pass are enormously strengthening to both the musculature and the joints. Their gymnastic value is the finest. The body development of the horse is unsurpassed by other exercises, and adding to this the magnificent test of balance, skills of spinal alignment along with proper lateral bend, we cannot match its value. Engagement is maximized by half- and full passes. Uniquely, they can be done in all three gaits.

The pirouette or portions of one (half, quarter or an eighth) maximize the horse's longitudinal engagement. It does this by emphasizing the "sitting on the haunches" by visibly lowering the croup, tucking and rounding the lumbar back and sinking on the joints of the haunches until the energetic movement is collected onto a spot not larger than a steak platter on which the hind legs turn. The liberty of the shoulders is not only developed, but is also tested by this most collected of the two-track movements. The elevation of the forehand is indispensable for pirouette work. This movement is based on maximum strength in the hocks and lower back, and is a test of strength and skill in maintaining perfect balance. Pirouettes can be done only at the walk and at the canter. While in both of these gaits they represent the highest degree of collection asked in tests, they make very different use of the muscles and joints, depending on which gait is performed. Pirouettes at the trot are sometimes performed by rotating a horse in the piaffe. This must only be done by master riders for it can cause harm if done incorrectly. The piaffe is not really a trot in place as much as it ought to be called a passage in place. I tend to think of an advanced horse's extended trot also rather as the most elongated passage. A true extended trot, just like a truly collected piaffe on the spot, should carry the majestic lift and suspension so typical of the passage. When rotating a horse at the piaffe, this suspension can sometimes be increased and the elevation of the forehand better secured. In the hands of a master, the horse can be greatly helped toward perfection of engagement that is delivered by the horse manifested with beauty and grace.

Thirteen

The Horse at the Canter

At the canter the horse is most "horselike." Everything we are aware of has definitive characteristics. These characteristics are the features by which we distinguish and recognize concepts. They are the features by which even those "primitive to the subject" can understand and recognize a concept. Anyone who knows the concept "horse" knows that nature designed him to canter. Definitive characteristics are those essential to things or ideas. The canter is essential to the horse. For the horse survived in nature by flight. He fled dangers such as fire and predators by cantering. He could maintain himself as a member of a herd. The herd could swiftly scatter or regroup for whatever reason. Horses live by cantering, survive by cantering and their anatomy is evolved by nature for cantering. Looking at the horse in terms of his skeletal, muscular, neurological, and sensory mechanisms, we can verify that he is by nature a "cantering organism" par excellence.

The horse feels most comfortable in traversing territory when doing it at the canter. Walking is for chores, including feeding. Transportation is by cantering and horses know that instinctively. Their body yields to that. When startled, they take off cantering. When hoping to dump the unwelcome burden of the unfriendly or unwittingly clumsy rider, they canter. Whenever they are feeling good, express joy, want to play, they do it at the canter. No horse is giddy at the walk or trot, let alone at the halt. Horses often sleep while standing at the halt. But when they "function," they do it best at the canter.

The cantering horse is beautiful. It takes a clumsy rider to spoil that. There are some people, even authorities in genetics, who believe that the trot is at best a late-developed gait and "at worst" possibly even man made! Meaning that horses started to trot at the end of their evolutionary process at about the time when man domesticated them and started to "guide" their genetics by selective breeding. If the trot is "man made," it is because horse owners for thousands of years favored the breeding of those members of the species that showed an aptitude to perform this seldom-seen action. The trot was, perhaps, an intermediate gait by which nature helped slow the galloping horse down toward his walk or halt. The trot may have been "the brakes." Certainly it is not a gait to be sustained for a prolonged period of time, according to the evidence that the horse's physiology presents.

Currently, much training is done at the trot. There are many reasons for this, among them that riders feel "safer" at a gait that does not remind the horse of his aptitude for flight from his enemies. Also, at the trot there is measured visual elegance, hypnotic floating pleasure in motion, metronomic regularity for the pleasure of the dancer in us all. The trot is a "cultured movement," and much of riding is focused on developing the horse well beyond the limits that he considers sufficient for a contented life. We are dedicated to maintaining the natural horse in his natural gaits under the foreign, stressful presence of the rider. Yet we are dedicating the art of riding to the extension of the horse's serviceable life and usefulness to man. Because of this, the art of riding is challenged by developing in each horse the very maximum of his natural potentialities. Since horses do have a potential for trot, we are very concerned with developing it to its maximum perfection, well beyond the gait the horse would volunteer by himself but never beyond its natural purity and correct expression!

I want to show nothing more with these photographs than that I still ride with great joy and that my life's pleasures include easy access to the Pacific Ocean's beaches and its sunsets.

I am riding, for the very first time, an old horse. We both found obvious pleasure in spending an evening on a splendid beach, waiting for the sun to set. Mostly we walked and cantered. I insisted on sparing my friend the trot at his age. The walk and the canter are friends of the horse. I tried to be also. Photos: Aggie Horn.

Nevertheless, those who know horsemanship will know that its beginnings are often spent in the great outdoors and not in the confines of the manege. There, the horse canters often by his own volition, "rolling it" from the trot as his enthusiasm of motion fills him. Indeed, horsemanship does not start with restraining. Young horses must be allowed forward, and better-schooled horses must be asked never to forget to move forward. The canter is potentially the fastest and therefore the most forward gait of them all. It is also an indispensable training tool and often the joy of the horse's working life.

At the walk the horse may learn easiest the "language" of his rider. Learn the aids, decipher them and acquire skills that are difficult and special. At the trot the horse may give pleasure to the rider, and may create floating images thrilling to the observer. But the horse "lives" at the canter.

Horses improve their respiration at the canter. Without that there can be no cross-country or jumping performance. The horse is "legged up" at the canter to make his limbs strong for working under the added weight of his rider. At the canter the horse "muscles up" those great articulated muscles on his haunches and flanks. The horse becomes an athlete at the canter! He may be used, tested and displayed and educated in the other gaits, but his athletic powers are born of the canter.

The young horse, in the natural environment, under his courageous and wise rider, will canter a lot. The well-schooled, accomplished athletic horse developed to or close to his genetic potentialities will be warmed up for competition at the canter by his wise rider. Both the simplest limbering and the most demanding collection succeed best at the canter.

The trot wears the horse down; the canter, on the other hand, tends to build him up. What we "build" at the canter is often "spent" at the trot. The canter saves the horse while the trot spends him.

Be sure to learn how to sit the canter correctly. When judging, I seldom see a rider sitting the canter correctly, even at the FEI levels! I see it even less when people come for coaching. Little is taught about equitation these days because we live in the age of the superhorse that tolerates the minimal rider. We have bred horses that can work in spite of their riders. They do not need aids (help) to do well because their talent shines for a while, even when hindered.

Once you can sit the canter correctly (deep, adhesive, and balanced), then use it to grow with your horse toward mutual perfection. What a vision a schooled canter is! The beauty of bounding energy in the motion, yet so slow that the rider floats on it and a ground person can stroll by his side. Without speed and hurry, the contained energies of the brilliant canter convey the ideal of horsemanship: energy in reserve for speedy flight, yet contained in tranquility to a slow majesty that will rest the mind of horse and rider in the same world of dreamlike weightlessness.

WAYS TO IMPROVE THE CANTER

The canter is one of the two "ancient" gaits, the walk is the other. The ancestors of the modern horse walked while feeding or at leisure and cantered when fleeing from danger. The evolutionary development of the trot came much later, and physiologically the trot is the least suitable, most wearing gait for the horse.

When evaluating a horse as a riding prospect, remember that usually a horse with a good natural walk will also have a fine canter, and vice versa. However, horses might show a splendid trot in spite of a mediocre walk and canter, or show a poor trot in spite of a wonderful walk and canter. In other words, walk and canter are consistently interrelated in quality, but trot remains by itself with its independent standard of quality. The trot, as an evolutionary latecomer, can also be developed to various qualitative heights of perfection, rather independent of the standards for the canter and walk.

On occasion we hear comments from riders that they have a young horse that cannot canter yet, and after inquiries it turns out to be five or six years old. Well, nature causes horses to canter sooner than it causes them to trot. A day-old foal will canter and frisk. Horses need to canter.

There are great canter preventers. They are not by the horse's choice, nor are they good for the horse. But they do prevent cantering. One reason for avoiding the canter is the rider's reasonable and well-founded fear of cantering. Knowing that he lacks adequate controls and balance, he naturally fears the canter. And so he should. For fear of falling is one of the basic fears and even thought by some scientists to be inborn. It certainly is one of the two fears observed in infants, the other being that of loud noises. Riders should not canter before they have a secure, balanced seat and beyond that well-honed skills to control the horse. The horse also needs guidance as to his balance, speed, bending, patterning, etc., and cannot be allowed to "improvise" the canter in a manege!

The young, unbalanced and stiff horse should not be asked to canter in a small manege. Confined spaces with corners that demand sharp turns (90 degrees or less!) are not suitable for young horses that have not yet found their natural balance under the added weight of the rider. Such horses ought to be allowed to canter on long straight paths out in the countryside. They would be better ridden by accomplished riders! In short, the green horse and the green rider ought not to canter. The two together, confined in a small space, often thought to be safe because it is small and fenced, do not make a good combination for cantering. To be sure, in a manege, in any confined space with corners, only a balanced, fairly supple horse should be permitted to canter and then only under a rider with a balanced, independent, deep and adhesive seat!

For the horse, however, cantering is easier than trotting. It is also less wearing on the joints, ligaments and muscular systems. On advanced horses, wise riders even warm up at the canter before wearing the horses out at the trot.

Unlike at the trot and walk, at the canter the horse uses his sides differently. In trot and walk, identical action on both sides of the horse is forthcoming, but not at the canter. Therefore, the canter is a lateral movement all the time, even when ridden straight ahead on a straightened horse. The limbs with their joints and muscles are differently used on either side of the horse in canter. This gait suggests to the horse to move with a slightly curved spine, throwing his haunches somewhat inward or leaning with the outside shoulder somewhat outward. Being crooked by "escaping" weight-bearing responsibilities with the inside

Susan Derr Drake is riding Will Power to show the difference between right and left lead canters. The canter is the only gait that is "unilateral" rather than "bilateral." The horse uses his inside differently than his outside even when progressing on a straight line. The canter actually has seven slightly different, discernible phases but always is in "three hoof beats" separated by a period of suspension. The magnitude of the suspension, the "bounding" of the horse, is most essential to the brilliance of the gait. At the right-lead canter (above left) the horse is in the very first phase of the "unit" of one canter bounding. This is the way the canter actually starts from any other gait! The outside hind leg assumes all the weight (impacting on the ground) while the other three legs are suspended above the ground.

The left-lead canter is in a later phase within the "bounding unit" of the stride. Both photographs clearly show why the lead is designated right or left. On the designated side the horse's forehand lifts the knee high and advances it ahead of (leading!) the outside forehand, which stays lower and behind. Photos: Paul Drake.

hind leg, and "escaping" by leaning outward and drifting to the outside shoulder, the horse can evade engagement.

Not unlike humans, horses are clever and efficient about escaping any work that they are not strongly shepherded to do. Eternally lazy, as all of us creatures are, horses will attempt to escape hard work. While horses cannot know, we do know that rehabilitation, physiotherapy and athletic progress all depend on the will to work a little harder beyond the comfort zone. We must have the will and the tact and the skills to convince horses of that. They in turn, having been improved, strengthened, suppled and better balanced, will have a new, improved comfort zone in which they will find a new efficiency that caters to their laziness. Much like human athletes, horses will progress gradually and carefully to new heights of athletic prowess and with each day of progress ought to become less desirous of evading their work.

There are few concepts almost synonymous with the goals of classical horsemanship. Of these, perhaps the most important is the admonition to "straighten your horse and ride it forward." We are advised to make a naturally one-sided creature ambidextrous. Only a straight horse can move forward, because "forward" does not refer to speed and flight but rather to the equal and sufficient loading of both hind legs! Conversely, only a horse that is strengthened and exercised to the efficiency that allows him to support evenly with his two hind legs can really straighten his spine. Again, the concept of "straightness" is not meant to be literal. It refers to the horse's ability to bend his spine evenly and continuously over the pattern on which he moves. A "straight" horse moving on a 20m circle has his spine bent exactly to the curvature of that circle, parallel with the pattern, beneath it.

"Straighten your horse and ride it forward" is the most difficult task at the canter, which is naturally not an ambidextrous movement. The horse's sides, on either side of his spine, must move dissimilarly. Yet we must achieve cantering on both leads with the same muscular and skeletal efficiency. A horse that canters dissimilarly on his two-canter leads is not yet ambidextrous, not yet "straight and forward."

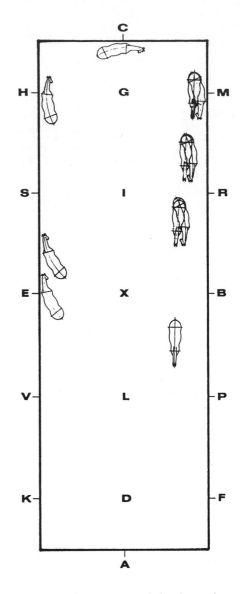

If you allow the horse to start the canter with his haunches in, you have made a big mistake. Horses, especially after they have been introduced to lateral work, will choose to interpret the rider's outside leg pressure for the canter departure as a suggestion for a haunches-in. This allows the horse to do the classic canter evasion of engagement by throwing his haunches inward while leaning his weight toward the outside shoulder.

In the illustration on page 162, such a departure is shown at E. Often riders pull the horse's head and shoulder toward the wall, and since the horse's hips are wider than his shoulders, the rider unwittingly forces the horse's haunches inward to avoid physically scraping the rail.

The horse can not easily be held "in the corridor" of leg and seat and reins. For in the naturally lateral canter gait, the rider's outside leg must be farther back than his vertically placed inside leg. Both reins also behave dissimilarly. All this makes straightening a difficult task that can most effectively be done by repeatedly riding the evasive horse's shoulder-fore—that is, by bringing his shoulders and therefore his withers inward enough to align the inside shoulder directly in front of the inside hip. The rider should not attempt to push the horse's evasive haunches back out with his inside leg—especially not by bringing his inside leg back. That would put him on his outside seatbone and signal a flying change. A crooked horse is certainly not ready for a flying change. If the horse is not ready for a flying change, this kind of attempt to straighten him will later confuse him when we do need to convey "flying change" with the inside leg pressing backward and inward.

The most reasonable training solution for straightening the canter and properly engaging the horse's haunches is based on proper patterning exercises. Properly applied patterns are, indeed, the most effective gymnastic strategies. All patterns are guided by reason. As in all crafts and arts, in riding too one must learn the appropriate patterns for remedying problems.

A horse that habitually departs into canter with his haunches thrown in should be prepared for each departure by a brief episode of shoulder-in. Depending on the level of training or other special needs under consideration, the shoulder-in can be done either at the walk or at the trot. For accuracy, improved balance and increased obedience, the departure should be done from the walk. For improving impulsion and greater elevation and rounding of the back, preparation should be done at the trot.

If the horse can deal with some collection, corrective measures can be practiced by departing the canter on a 10m circle. On the circle, one ought to pay attention to prevent possible "overcurving" inward with the haunches.

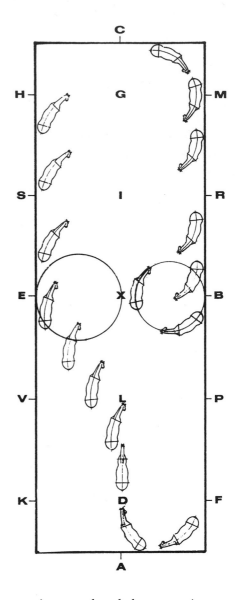

Once the transitions are improved and the canter is proceeding, one should straighten the horse by bringing the inside shoulder in front of the inside hind leg. Never push the haunches outward to "line them up" behind the shoulders. This latter approach does not succeed because of the inherent nature of the unilateral seat and aids required for the canter. Such actions might cause rushing, a flying change or tension at the jaw. By looking at the illustration (opposite) again and seeing the horse at M, one notices that the horse's crookedness is being corrected by bringing his inside shoulder inward to be aligned with his inside hip. If he throws the haunches inward again, the rider continues to repeat the same corrective action. In a short while the horse will abandon his evasions and become obedient by surrendering his inside hind leg to its proper weight-bearing and propelling functions. When one distances from the wall by these exercises, one can return to the wall with a plié, which is both corrective and strengthening and, in this case, serves well as a complement to the earlier shoulder-fore procedures.

THE PLIÉ AND ITS USES

We discussed the plié earlier, but it is important to mention here that the term, as many others in the equestrian arts, is borrowed from the world of ballet. Yet plié means something vastly different in riding than in ballet. The plié can help in the following important efforts:

- It always helps engage the haunches of the cantering horse, thereby improving the rider's control over the haunches and the horse's understanding of how to collect the canter properly. It is a great skill-building and body-building exercise for the horse.
- The plié also improves the horse's obedience to the straightening and collecting aids of his rider. It improves the horse's balance and fosters the shifting of the center of gravity backwards which equals, of course, collection. It straightens the crooked horse at the canter; it will help the horse to understand how his shoulders are controlled by the rider and therefore provides preparatory work even for the pirouettes (hence, the original, ballet-related meaning of plié!).

The plié is a shoulder-in–like movement in the canter. The degree to which the horse's shoulders are positioned inward can vary somewhat. The minimum degree of inward positioning is the ideal one in which we merely bring the horse's inside shoulder flush with the inside hip. Increasing the angulation inward is not ideal but an often necessary exaggeration when there is a need for severe corrective action.

Patterns for Plié

Because of the plié's great importance in perfecting canter work, I want to discuss some elementary patterns for teaching and practicing plié.

First ride the horse correctly bent through a 10m half-circle from F to D and there straighten him for one stride as shown in the illustration on page 164. This is a wonderful experience for both horse and rider, although it is not easy and requires advanced skills. Its purpose is to prevent the horse from drifting toward his outside shoulder and "rubber-necking" inward after the turn down the center line. Then begin "drifting" diagonally outward from D to E, making sure that the shoulders are controlled to remain "upright" and not allowing the shoulders to bulge and that the inside hind leg (the right in this illustration) is well engaged. By using more of the rider's inside shoulder driving downward-forward into the inside seat, and by activating with the inside leg, one increases the "inside coordinate's demand" while receiving and balancing the excesses with the outside rein. A sense of collection will occur, with a feeling of a taller horse that moves with more gracefully elevated strides, better engaged and freer at the shoulders.

Arriving at the wall by E, one has several options to choose from, depending on feel and identification of further needs. One might opt, for instance, to ride a 20m or 10m circle in order to lose any tension and stretch and round the topline by elevating the back and sinking the mid-neck. One might even gradually lengthen the rein and stretch the horse's neck forward and down during such circles. On the other hand, one might choose to ride on straight for the rest of the wall to verify the success of the straightening procedure. Or, one might continue from E to H with the shoulder-fore and increase collection!

Once the plié has served its purpose and taught the horse

obedience, improved balance, strength, etc., we ought to discontinue its frequent use. This diagonally drifting pattern is fundamentally a teaching, schooling exercise for both horse and rider, not a movement to retain to show the horse's accomplishments during any evaluative performances (i.e., competition). There are many schooling movements one ought not to continue to use as means to achieving an end after the ends we sought have been well established.

Again, patterns that involve a plié are infinite in potential variety. Use your inventiveness and imagination. Remember that the horse will tell you when you have overphased him or ill-used the plié by illogical patterning. Horses verify by confirming when we are right!

THE COUNTER CANTER

The counter canter is one of the crucial exercises for perfecting the horse's balance and it is essential in the training of jumping and cross-country horses as well as those horses whose performance remains in the dressage arena. Primarily, counter canter creates collection, provided that it is not just a canter on the wrong lead. Of course, not all canters delivered on the outside lead qualify as counter canter; in some cases the horse is performing on the wrong lead. The difference is in the balance. When the center of gravity increases toward the haunches, counter canter is clearly achieved.

The counter canter, as opposed to being on the wrong lead, is initiated by the rider rather than being a disobedience from the horse. We must be sure that the horse's bending remains toward his lead. If he proceeds along the wall or on a circle, a counter flexion, opposite the direction toward which we progress will become necessary. The bending of the horse toward the direction of his canter lead must be identical to the bending he would offer when on the true lead! If a horse is cantering on the right lead, for instance, he must be slightly bent toward the right (when along straight lines, merely "positioned" toward the lead). Regardless of how many times one changes direction alternating from "true" to "counter" canter, the horse remains on the right lead, bent slightly to the right. The degree of bending must not increase or decrease when the horse changes direction, but should remain consistently identical regardless of the direction of progress. This progressional direction is the single determining factor in whether a canter is on the true or on the counter lead. As mentioned before, whenever a horse is laterally bent inward, in accordance with the direction of progress, he is in a true figure. Whenever he is asked to bend opposite from the direction of his progression, we label the movement a "counter" figure.

The counter canter, beyond rebalancing horses toward improved collection, strengthens the horse's lumbar region (lower back) and helps tuck the pelvis under. Riding the canter in the true lead also encourages this, but it is the rider's skill and the horse's level of obedience that determine whether the attempted development succeeds. However, when riding a counter canter the strengthening and tucking of the lower back becomes an indispensable necessity, done "automatically" by the horse who cannot otherwise perform the canter on the outside lead and in good balance and impulsion. Therefore, "the pattern is allowed to work the horse" in addition to the indispensable helping aids of the rider.

During counter canter particularly, the hips are asked to articulate more and carry more stress, strengthening and suppling as a consequence. It it a fabulous body-building exercise because the horse's musculature must work well beyond the comfort zone afforded by cantering on the true lead.

The counter canter can easily be introduced to horses in this way: Instead of riding straight along the long wall of the manege, leave the wall, let us say at H, and guide the horse slightly inward with outside leg, "peeling him off the wall" toward the quarter line (5m away from the wall). When reaching the quarter line, change the aids to "displace" the horse outward back to the wall, reaching it at about K. This mild single-loop, flat serpentine line can be made more sophisticated by various elaborations as the horse progresses in understanding, balance and strength. One certainly should begin to suggest sideways movements on two tracks, making the H to the quarter line portion into a half-pass left as much as possible and making the quarter line to returning to K portion a plié. When that improves, one can carry the two-

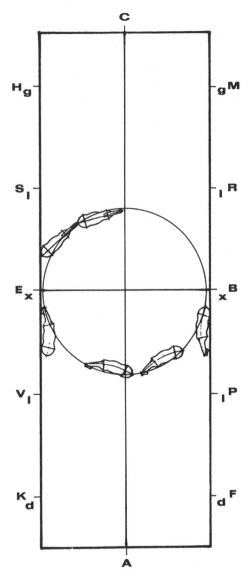

Observe that the counter canter is only correct and gymnastically valid (useful) if the horse is kept tracking right over the pattern with both hind and front legs. His hind legs must continue forward in the direction of his forehands. And if one changes on a figure-8 from counter canter to an equal-sized circle to ride a true canter, one should not change the horse's bending. In short, do not permit the horse to overbend laterally toward the lead.

The evasions of engagement in the counter canter are based precisely on the horse exaggeratedly throwing his haunches outward, off the pattern (here a circle), or over-positioning his shoulder and neck outward into an exaggerated bending toward the lead. These evasions, at E and B respectively, are nullifying the counter canter and making the movement merely a horse on the wrong lead.

Past E progressing toward the center line are the two common faults a horse would make when kept too straight, without any lateral bending toward the lead. He will either fall outward with his haunches or cut inward with his shoulder, relative to the path of progress. The two examples near the center line progressing from B to E are correct: counter canter with mild outward (toward the lead) lateral bending and with poll and tailbone placed on the arc of the circle.

track values to greater sophistication by tracking all the way to the center line and changing from half-pass to plié at X.

Returning to the original single-loop serpentine without any two-tracks, merely going from H to quarter line to K, one can elaborate in another direction, without the two-track movements and remain on single track, yet with counter-canter episodes increasing. Using these strategies, one would simply ride the horse gradually farther away from (H–K) long wall as he improves, and finally reach the other wall around B. Then ride him back toward K and achieve a three-loop serpentine without changing lead. The second of the three loops is at the center line.

After we have succeeded with a short episode of counter canter on a three-loop serpentine that progressed from wall to wall, we can work on it in earnest. Make the first and last loops smaller for collection because the horse is has an "easier time" at the true canter during them. At the counter canter, however, one makes the loop middle rather large, to make it comfortable and therefore possible for the horse not to alter the quality of his canter from the true to the counter. Rhythm is very important. When teaching and practicing the counter canter it is essential that the rhythm remain unchanged from that of the true canter. If the horse rushes, it is a sure sign of loss of balance that can be dealt with by appropriate corrective measures too numerous to detail here. But the most important corrective measure at all times regarding all exercises is to revisit the old, familiar, known ways and give the horse more time to prepare and mature to the performance of the task at hand. A severe loss of balance during counter canter certainly suggests the revisitation of collection in the true canter and a more gradual, careful start with counter canter on easier patterns, such as the single, flat serpentine one started on.

The greatest difficulties emerge when riders come to the crowning pattern of the confirmed, sophisticated counter canter: performing it on circles.

The counter canter is an exercise that helps perfect the horse's balance, strengthens the back muscles, particularly behind the saddle, and establishes utmost obedience to the rider's aids. Thus it is important to note that this exercise improves the horse's mentality, his musculature and his skeleton. Muscle, of course, moves skeleton. But we are always concerned with skeletal balance and the strength and suppleness of the joints.

In counter canter, the hind legs of the horse must continue to move toward the hoofprints of the forelegs, exactly as they do in true canter. When performing the counter canter on a circle or an arc, the hind legs must track on the prescribed arc and under no circumstances deviate inward or outward from the pattern. Nor should the forelegs track off to the inside or outside of the prescribed arc. In short, both forelegs and the hind legs following them must remain on the pattern.

As the horse must maintain a continuous, mild bend toward the lead at the counter canter on the circle, he will not parallel the arc of the circle with his spinal column. Rather, he will be counter-flexed. Yet this must be so mild, that while maintaining his balance in collection, only his neck is slightly bent away from the circular arc to the outside.

Common Problems in the Counter Canter

There are several common mistakes that must be avoided in the counter canter. For example, the horse may cross-canter or change lead when asked to perform a counter canter on the circle. In fact, often teaching a flying change of lead is done from a counter canter on a circle to the inside lead and continuing in the true canter as a "reward" for having done the flying change. However, to avoid an unwanted and uncalled-for flying change,

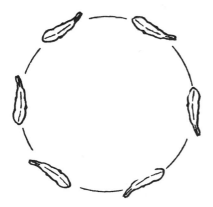

one must increase the emphasis on the rider's correct aids. All aids must be in place, and slightly more effective but most important is the effectiveness of the rider's outside leg. That leg must maintain the horse's engagement and vigor to "jump through" with good impulsion. The rider's shoulder, hip and leg positions must remain impeccable to maintain correct center of gravity. The rider must always parallel the horse's shoulders with his own shoulders and the horse's hips with his own pelvis. Seldom is it more important than in the counter canter to be absolutely meticulous about these relationships and about bending the horse with the legs and not by steering manipulations with the reins.

A rider lacking such skills should not attempt to school a horse in the counter canter, for his efforts would only be counterproductive. Thus, the desired form consists of outside leg back with heel down, calf stretched, leg wrapped onto the horse's ribcage and not bouncing; inside leg perpendicular, allowing the horse to bend around it an also providing rhythmic impulsion; the rider's inside shoulder leading exactly as does the horse's, ensuring that the rider is on the inside seatbone, with light rhythmic following through a yielding inside rein. The inside hand must never pull the head to create flexion. The outside hand remains offered steadily for the horse to contact.

In this discussion, "inside" refers to the side of the horse that is hollowed by the contraction of muscles, the "outside" being the longer, stretched side. "Inside" refers to the side on which the leading leg works, while the outside, of course, has the "starting hind leg" for each canter stride. Consequently, the horse's "outside" will be toward the center of the circle on which the counter canter progresses.

A common problem with the counter canter is centered on the horse's evasion of collection by throwing his haunches outward off the circular track, not following toward the hoofprints of his forelegs. This would put the haunches outward, off the circular track, not following toward the hoofprints of his forelegs. To discourage this error, be sure that you school the horse on an arc sufficiently large for him to cope with at his stage of gymnastic development. Never forget that the horse is your calendar. He verifies his progress. If it is not forthcoming, we must retrace our steps and make the exercises easier than proposed.

To begin with, ride a circle in the true canter and observe the horse's mild inward bending, level of engagement, energy, rhythm and balance. Observe the energy of strides, the clarity of bounding suspension in the movement. Then simply change direction and ride the same size circle, while maintaining the original lead, to gain your counter canter. With advanced horses this is possible even on 10m circles, but with beginning horses one must do nothing smaller than 20m circles.

If the horse's neck is allowed to bend more than the rest of his body, the exercise becomes harmful. As a matter of principle,

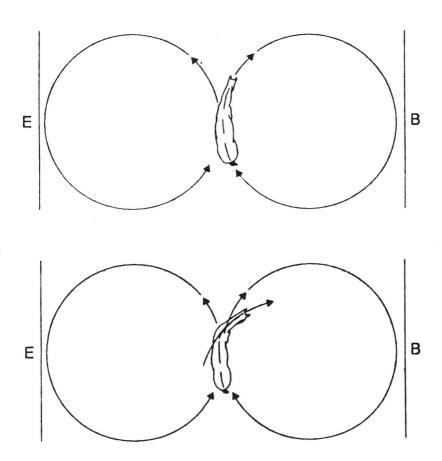

overbending the neck is always a severe fault. It shows the rider does not understand one of the essentials of classical equitation: that the horse's neck must be controlled always and only at the base of the neck. That is, we control the whereabouts of the shoulders and withers and let the neck issue forth from there, as if the reins were always held in one fist only. Riders who wish to control the outer end of the neck, that is the horse's muzzle, lose control of the continuous bend and, with it, totally lose control of the whereabouts of the haunches. In addition to that greatest of harm, the riders who overbend the horse's neck inhibit the all-important (because of weight-bearing responsibilities) work of the inside hind leg. Hands should only control but never inhibit the freedom of the horse's limbs, nor should the hands shape the horse's neck. The horse should always feel free to carry his neck where the haunches place it and to hang his head from the poll wherever it is naturally carried.

Premature attempts to collect the horse on a circle in counter canter can result in loss of balance that could produce anything from a slight hurry to a scampering rush. If this happens, the horse begins to lean toward his outside shoulder to compensate for the lack of balance. Instead, he should always remain perpendicularly upright during counter canter.

Finally, the worst mistake happens when a horse is allowed to lose his correct bending and counter canter in "counter flexion," that is, to canter with his neck bent opposite from the

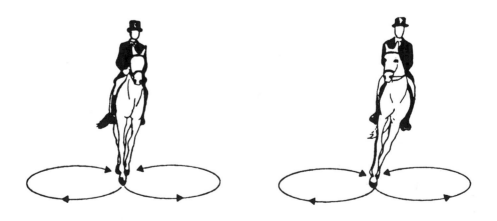

side of his leading foreleg. The horse is struggling in the wrong lead to balance in an S-curve through his spine.

Remember that while schooling horses and gymnasticizing them, there is no neutrality. One either improves them or they are in a process of breaking down. There is no "holding pattern" or "coasting along" and there is no "wait a minute" in horsemanship. One either builds or destroys the horse without a third alternative!

Analogous to this principle concerning the horse's physical condition is the principle that there is no time during the schooling of a horse when he is not learning something. A good rider makes sure that his horse is learning desirable things and makes habits of them. However, there is never a time when the rider can suspend learning and tell the horse "I did not mean that," or "Wait a minute while I sort this out." The horse learns everything that is practiced on him and by him. As a consequence, much "negative learning" occurs if horses are trained by ignorant riders. For the horse does not know the difference between "good" and "bad" and merely becomes efficient, rather than proficient, at whatever his rider schools him to do. Many horses, therefore, learn to excel at horrible mistakes. They do it with goodwill and jollity, for they aim to please, even though they may feel uncomfortable or in pain.

Sophisticated riders will not start schooling the impossible, will not school "movements" before the horse is ready to perform them. Good riders will not pursue "movements" to fulfill some esoteric competition requirement. They will, rather, school their horse to become a great gymnast and execute his basic gaits correctly—then, incidentally, perhaps compete.

Before doing counter-canter, horses must be able to collect the canter somewhat. They should also be able to travel on two tracks in half-pass and plié. Every movement and every schooling pattern has its own developmental history. We always start with meager beginnings. We hope to reach, eventually, gradually and patiently, near ideals. And those guiding ideals will always elude us. And that is equestrian life and equestrian effort.

Fourteen

Canter Patterns for Gymnastic Advancement

The canter pattern explained at the very beginning of counter-canter work is a very important one. In addition to its introductory uses, it should have a life of its own and remain with us throughout our training strategies. The great value in this exercise, which is to half-pass inward from the beginning of the long wall and return to the end of the same wall by means of a plié, is that the horse remains on the same lead, with the same amount of bend and positioning. Yet the rider must alternately displace the horse first with his outside, then with his inside leg without changing his center of gravity. In short, the rider's position is unchanged, the horse's position is unchanged. Yet the horse's direction of travel and the emphasis on weight-bearing of the hind legs change. The horse's inside hind leg bears the weight throughout, but in half-pass his outside hip, in plié his inside hock, gain the greatest suppling.

One possible elaboration, as in most cases when using two-track movements, is the insertion of a circle. After a few strides at the half-pass, one could circle, then continue with plié. The advantage of the circle is always the same: It reestablishes the correct basics if they become compromised by the "figures."

The circle gives horse and rider a chance to iron out difficulties, to regain balance, collection, impulsion, suspension and all the good things that define an improved and well-schooled basic gait.

One can also canter on a 20m circle left. Diminish the circle until the horse feels collected sufficiently to influence the outside hind leg to step under him enough to create a half-pirouette and proceed away from the half-pirouette with a half-pass to the left.

This exercise offers great advantages, among them that the rider does not lose control of the haunches. Allowing the shoulders to "cut in," or lean inward, and letting the haunches "spin out," would, however, render this exercise useless. Also, impulsion can be regained during the half-pass because it tends to liberate the forehand and allows the shoulders great freedom. Following a half- (or later a full) pirouette with a half-pass prevents flying changes or cross cantering as the rider's preparatory behavior disallows either.

Very much depends on the quality of each movement and on which movement follows it, because the rider's preparatory behavior toward the next movement often defines the very quality of the ongoing movement. Riding is very dynamic: it is an ongoing process. No movement or exercise is by itself. All must be prepared for and concluded carefully. How movements are prepared for or concluded is critical. Therefore, the intelligence in the strategy of combinations of movements elevates the art of riding to one of the most complex of scholarly activities, yet one utterly dependent on imagination and an attitude toward invention and novelty that encourages varied but always logical schooling.

To school the half-pass, a useful pattern is to canter from K to the center line to the right in half-pass. Then drive on straight and turn right at C. Then repeat by half-passing from M to the center line and proceed straight to A. One can, of course, elaborate by adding a circle to the right at the center line before straightening onto the center line. This, however, could encourage the horse to "cut in" with the inside shoulder. Concluding half-passes by straightening the horse, aligning his hindquarters once again with his shoulders, is absolutely one of the most important tasks. Poorly concluded half-passes, that fall into

Susan Derr Drake is riding Will Power at the canter in a half-pass to the right. Notice that the location of the photographer makes it appear as if the horse were leading with his haunches. Far from it, when viewed from front center. Indeed, I asked for a picture from this difficult angle to show that the horse in the canter half-pass progresses sideways without straddling or crossing his legs. He progresses sideways in the suspension period by displacing himself in the "bounding" episode of suspension. This illustrates a great difference in the meaning and purpose of this movement from those half-passes at the walk and the trot where the straddling of legs is essential.

Therefore, at the canter the balancing and collection values are the highest. At the trot and the walk it is the suppling of the hips and shoulders. Photo: Paul Drake.

circles or turns, can cause trouble. On a well-schooled horse, one can dare a circle left at the counter canter. If this counter-canter circle is only 10m left of the center line (on the right lead canter), it is very difficult test of great collection. However, if the half-pass were allowed to continue all the way across the school from one long wall to the other, the circle could be 20m and easier at the counter canter. Once the counter canter is introduced as an elaboration, the combinations offer endless possibilities. For one can continue with serpentines, figure-8s and repeated returns to the half-pass at the true canter. The results can be gymnastically sensational because these exercises collect, supple and elasticize as few others can.

When cantering, of course, the same general training principles apply as in the trot or walk. One of the most important of these principles is that every pattern ridden in collection should be followed by another at extension and vice versa. However small or great the degree of collection or extension, elasticity and obedience will only improve if these two concepts are constantly interchanged and alternated during training.

After a collected canter exercise, try turning down the center line at A on the left lead and from the center line canter "outward" to M, giving the horse a longer straight path than the long wall offers. Extend the strides on this long path. If the same pattern is pursued as a plié, it will serve the cause of collection, of course. Never extend at the plié. Extensions are for single-track movements.

More sophisticated, for the advanced horse, can be a counter canter pursued around the perimeter of the manege. Then, turn down the center line; on the right lead counter canter at A and half-pass to the long wall. From there go on straight until you can turn onto the center line at C and repeat half-passing "outward" to the right. This is a wonderful suppling exercise. It starts with a small 10m half-circle at the counter canter (between the long wall and center line) and "releases tension" as it were, by half-passing outward, away from the stress point on the center line toward the long wall with the now true-canter half-pass. This half-pass can also be controlled with regard to the degree of angulation toward the wall. The more sideways the half-pass is, the more "schooled," slow and seated the canter becomes.

However, by allowing a more forward and less sideways pattern for the half-pass, we can encourage impulsion and freedom at the shoulders.

Another wonderful exercise sequence can be started from a counter canter along the wall. For example, ride a left lead counter canter to M and leave that wall by way of plié to X. From X half-pass back to the same wall to F. This is the "reverse" of the exercise we use to promote the learning of counter canter. This sequence of exercises reinforces more than the other the horse's awareness that he is ridden "between the rider's legs" and handlessly, both for collection and for displacement. Remain in left lead counter canter from F to the center line and turn onto it at A. Then ride an 8m circle if you dare to (or stay at 10m if you are not ready) and half-pass out to the wall on your left. You may continue with a number of options: either straight on or a flying change and then straight on. Or you can opt to continue collection at the counter canter but on a large 20m circle to "loosen things up," maybe even in a longer frame after the preceding taxing chain of exercises.

SCHOOLING CANTER PIROUETTES

One sees relatively few well-done canter pirouettes. Searching for the reasons for this, I have some observations to offer. One obvious reason for failing to perform a proper pirouette is simply that the horse is not yet ready to deliver it. Preparation is time-consuming and is based on expertise as well as on the riding skills that can actually make it happen. Often all three of these ingredients are missing. An unprepared, stiff, tense horse is brought to a short about-turn of bewildering quality by a rider out of balance and not even sitting properly.

Discounting such unfortunate sightings, one can observe the second important cause for problems with pirouettes. And this is the rider's or coach's misunderstanding that the pirouette is all about turning around the inside hind leg. Indeed, that is how it is delivered, but the pirouette is all about the ultimate collection of a very pure canter gait. There must be first and foremost nothing else at all but a horse in a pure canter gait with greatly energetic bounding suspension in the stride, yet so schooled to sit on the haunches that the canter is slow and slower and slowest, and the footfalls come down silently like snow. And then, one incidentally turns the horse on the spot to continue in another direction or turns around completely in a full pirouette.

Riders who remember that pirouettes are done at the school canter and are to manifest and prove collection will succeed. Those who think of it as turning a horse around will not.

Observing pirouette work, whether as a judge, a coach or just a bystander, one frequently sees that pirouettes to the left are too large. This is because the horse's hind legs cannot remain in a small area the size of a steak platter and consequently they often turn about on a good-size circle, or the haunches will skid outward, against the rider's outside leg. This latter problem may even cause a turn around the rider's torso with the horse's shoulders falling and cutting inward and the haunches spinning outward, so the horse turns around its center.

These troubled left pirouettes are then often "corrected" by an insistent rider who "puts them on a dime" but at the cost of counter flexing the horse, who may also come off the bit. Poor left pirouettes are often the result of an overzealous outside rein contact by the rider. This simultaneously discourages proper bending to the left and inhibits the outside hind leg, the all-important "starting" leg of each canter stride.

The only remedy is to school the horse until he is collected enough to obey the outside leg of the rider and to resist the temptation to use the outside rein for "collection" and for turning.

I have argued and advised against ever using the haunches-in at the canter. And least of all as a preparation for canter pirouette. In fact, canter pirouettes showing haunches-in on approach to or during the pirouette itself are as faulty to the degree as half-passes with haunches leading would be. For that is evasion and disengagement indeed! Instead one should use the spiraling inward with a shoulder-fore at the canter. The shoulder-in must be avoided at the canter because one must never permit the crossing of the horse's legs.

However, the shoulder-fore brings the horse's inside shoulder in line with his inside hip and consequently sets the outside shoulder well inward of his outside hip, since the hips are much wider than the shoulders. This engages the horse, activates the inside hock splendidly in the canter; and the withers are already somewhat in to commence the turning episode of the pirouette. The haunches will surely not evade their task by being thrown inward!

As the spiral tightens and the horse is maintained in shoulder-fore, his collection increases. The pirouette is not all about turning. It is all about collection. During the pirouette, the horse shows the greatest amount of collection he is capable of at the canter. Collection is improved by this spiraling exercise.

Once the horse is on the volte, the rider feels the readiness of his collection. He only needs to gently rotate around and there is the pirouette, with haunches lowering in the middle of the spiral. Then, spiral out, rather than dash forward, to teach the horse further collection and avoid the anticipated flying change or counter bending.

PATTERNS FOR CANTER PIROUETTES

Here are some pattern suggestions for the schooling of canter pirouettes.

Ride a right lead true canter along the wall to B. Make sure to establish good impulsion, suspension (bounding) and roundness through the topline of the horse. The horse's contact with the ground becomes soft and like liquid flows through the horse's body, and blankets it from the hocks to the bit. Then ask for some stronger, longer strides toward the corner to F. At the end of the short wall half-halt and continue in a collected canter. From K to B change rein either with a straight or a half-passing horse. Then begin a 20m circle on the counter canter, right lead, around X. Perform the counter canter a few times around X to increase engagement, build the balance toward the haunches, lighten the forehand and sense a "pelvic tucking" or "sinking feeling" behind you while the withers elevate taller. Make sure all the time that the horse is not evading by throwing his haunches outward or by overbending with the neck toward the lead. The horse should feel, even on contact, elevated through his rounded back and liquid through the neck. When feelings are correct, perform an "outward pirouette," that is, a pirouette (or a portion of one) to the right when crossing the center line. From there you could continue straight up the center line to elaborate with anything that is reasonable for improvement. One can ask for a straight, balanced halt to improve collection and obedience. One can walk away from it to a rest. One can go to the wall and challenge with an extended canter and do many more potentially good, continuing exercises.

By such exercises the pirouette will be well forecast and prepared for by the movements that precede it. The canter should remain very slow in rhythm, measured and cadenced. The pirouette itself should be utterly void of "retroactive hands," which is the proper, polite *terminus technicus* for "do not pull." The pirouette must be executed by the rider's seat and legs only and this can be verified by slackening the rein a little during its performance. The rider should feel adhesively seated with a "flowing" inside seat, thigh and deep heel position.

As in all two-track movements—and the pirouette is the epitome of them all—the beginning and end are crucial to their successful execution. To be sure the beginning is seated and the outside hind leg is working and the lumbar back is tucking, one can best school toward a pirouette through a half-pass. When the half- or full pirouette is completed, one can depart from it also in a half-pass. This prevents the shoulder from "overspinning" and makes sure the rider can "upright" the forehand through the movement. Therefore, both entering and exiting a pirouette via a half-pass is an excellent training strategy. The beginning depends on the rider's outside leg control of the haunches, and with half-pass there it is! The end depends on the control over the horse's shoulder. By aligning it with the haunches, one may successfully depart in the half-pass.

All riding is interrelated. Movements on two tracks, even more intimately so. But the half-pass and pirouette at the canter are even interdependent, beyond being just interrelated. I believe that collection and the resultant self-carriage are indispensable for both. To prove that you have it, you should be able to halt your horse at any stride of your choice during these most collected exercises. Not at the beginning of your schooling, however, but on an accomplished, well-exercised horse that is familiar with the movement and capable of handling it. One must time and again be able to stop in the very midst of a half-pass (especially at the trot!) and at the pirouette.

Nothing is more false than a horse "running off the leg" and going sideways just to drift away from rider-contact. The horse must remain between the aids, tolerate them first, accept them later, surrender to them and seek them ultimately. A horse that will not stop square and balanced on any stride of a half-pass or pirouette is not yet trained in these movements. Halt, of course, without pulling!

Fifteen

Patterns for Improving Flying Tempi Changes

Several patterns are useful for improving flying tempi changes. One can ride a collected canter along the perimeter of the manege (i.e., "go large") to avoid anticipation by and anxiety of the horse. Riding diagonals would be wise to avoid. Horses often associate diagonals with flying changes because they remember that they were schooled on diagonals and are shown there in competitions. Therefore, continue to pretend that you are just hacking around, but in a collected canter, as effortlessly and with as light rein contact as possible. During canter, yield with one hand forward to produce a loose contact on one side. Once established, this confirms and assures the self-carriage that is indispensable for active, collected canter. The hands, especially when wrongly used for contacting strongly, will inhibit the horse's strides and impede his ability to articulate with the joints, especially the hocks. We must remember that each hand has a strong and direct influence on the use of the hock on the same side.

The rider should have the mental attitude of riding straight along a path through a forest. In short, there should be no sense

Dr. Reiner Klimke on Ahlerich is taking the honor round after having won the individual and team Gold Medals at Los Angeles in the 1984 Olympics.

It is not so "lonesome at the top," as this picture suggests, because he was performing a seemingly endless number of flying canter changes on every stride while the crowd of tens of thousands roared their approval. Indeed, in ways more astonishing than his Gold Medal-winning, superb ride, the feat of taking his spirited horse calmly around in this thundering arena, performing hundreds of yards of flying changes every stride followed by hundreds of yards at the passage, was more breathtaking than anything else. As memories, they remain matchless and etched more deeply than any standard dressage test can ever be.

There is much to be learned from this picture that says "more than a thousand words." The horse is on his leading forehand ready to leave the earth for a period of suspension, during which he will change his lead to arrive on the other hind leg, alternating from the one before. Hence, the near parallel position of the two hind legs as the horse readies the "new outside" for the touchdown!

The horse is attentive yet calm, contrary to instinct, by being focused on his trusted rider, who happens to ask for dozens of the most difficult movements, flying changes on every stride. The horse is calm, his tail hanging. The rider smiles with joy, salutes his admirers with hat off, reins in one hand and still doing the flying changes on every stride.

Riders know how difficult it is to perform fifteen of these tempi changes, in silence, alone, with reins in both hands. Yet here, all was "easy." Had the Olympic test not won the Gold Medal for Dr. Klimke, this honor round should have. Photo: Thomas M. Baron.

that you are "setting something up," that you are preparing to "school by demand." Instead, concentrate on nothing else but traveling on a straight horse, moving calmly and very surely in self-carriage. Once you succeed with this goal, you can ask for an occasional change of lead, at first always at the convenience of the horse. That is, ask for a flying change when you are changing patterns and the horse would find cantering easier on the opposite lead.

When single changes come easily and without any change in balance and rhythm, you can plan on asking for flying changes in multiples, that is, on every fourth, third or second stride. Eventually, of course, on every stride. Flying changes on every stride are the ultimate proof of both obedience to the rider and the utmost coordination of the horse. This sophisticated exercise has drawn some debate as to its validity. Some experts argue that changing canter lead on every stride is an "artificial gait," as the horse does not fully complete any of the canter strides. However, it is a natural activity during canter even by horses free of riders and especially so when foals are skipping around.

When asking for flying changes at every certain number of strides, it would be wise to develop these changes along the short wall of the manege to insure automatically a stronger sense of collection toward the horse's haunches and to hint to the horse that speeding up on such a short wall and before a corner is, indeed, not profitable. The footing must be well prepared and level, and the corners must be ridden in balance with collection for this exercise.

Also a good idea remains the practicing of sequence changes on a large circle (20m diameter). Every horse jumps through to one side with greater ease and facility than to the other. Of course, the horse must then be ridden in canter on the circle in the direction that enables the easier flying change to be performed to the outside lead while the more difficult one is performed to the inside lead, thereby providing the rewarding relief of arriving on the true canter after a successful change.

When practicing or teaching the flying changes on every stride, the tempi changes, one ought to plan for three consecutive changes. The center line is a highly appropriate location for the teaching of this difficult coordination exercise. It allows the rider to monitor the horse's straightness better than when along a wall. Absolute straightness is essential, even crucial, to success. One should ask for the first and third flying change to go toward the easy lead and the second or middle stride to the more difficult side. Obviously, doing changes twice to the easy side and only once toward the hard one is logical. Doing only two consecutive flying changes can also be a wise strategy if they are done at a planned frequency. For instance, two changes on every stride being followed by four strides on the same lead before the next two consecutive changes are asked for. This way, one can take a calm horse around the school with varying strides before changes are called and allow him to learn to listen for the rider's calls rather than rush about anticipating his supposed actions.

In competition, tempi changes (changes on every stride) are asked for only on straight patterns, diagonals or center lines. However, in schooling, one ought to confirm their availability by asking a well-trained horse for their performance on a 20m circle.

Index